DILEMMAS

DILEMMAS

THE TARNER LECTURES
1953

BY

GILBERT RYLE

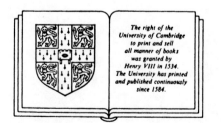

CAMBRIDGE UNIVERSITY PRESS
CAMBRIDGE
NEW YORK   NEW ROCHELLE   MELBOURNE   SYDNEY

Published by the Press Syndicate of the University of Cambridge
The Pitt Building, Trumpington Street, Cambridge CB2 1RP
32 EAST 57th Street, New York, NY 10022, USA
10 Stamford Road, Oakleigh, Melbourne 3166 Australia

ISBN C 521 06177 6 hard covers
ISBN 0 521 09115 2 paperback

First published 1954
Reprinted 1956
First paperback edition 1960
Reprinted 1962, 1964, 1966, 1969, 1973, 1975, 1976,
1977, 1980, 1983, 1985, 1987

Transferred to digital printing 2002

CONTENTS

I am very grateful to the Master and Fellows of Trinity College, Cambridge, for the honour they did me in electing me their twelfth Tarner Lecturer. This book is a slightly modified version of the Tarner Lectures which I delivered in Cambridge in the Lent Term of 1953.

G. R.

I

DILEMMAS

THERE are different sorts of conflicts between theories. One familiar kind of conflict is that in which two or more theorists offer rival solutions of the same problem. In the simplest cases, their solutions are rivals in the sense that if one of them is true, the others are false. More often, naturally, the issue is a fairly confused one, in which each of the solutions proffered is in part right, in part wrong and in part just incomplete or nebulous. There is nothing to regret in the existence of disagreements of this sort. Even if, in the end, all the rival theories but one are totally demolished, still their contest has helped to test and develop the power of the arguments in favour of the survivor.

However, this is not the kind of theoretical conflict with which we shall be concerned. I hope to interest you in quite a different pattern of disputes, and, therewith, in quite a different sort of settlement of these disputes.

There often arise quarrels between theories, or, more generally, between lines of thought, which are not rival solutions of the same problem, but rather solutions or would-be solutions of different problems, and which, none the less, seem to be irreconcilable with one another. A thinker who adopts one of them seems to be logically committed to rejecting the other, despite the fact that the inquiries from which the theories issued had, from the beginning, widely divergent goals. In disputes of this kind, we often find one and the same thinker—very likely oneself—strongly inclined to champion both sides and yet, at the very same time, strongly inclined entirely to repudiate one of them just because he is strongly inclined to support the other. He is both well satisfied with the logical credentials of each of the two points of view, and sure that one of them must be totally wrong if the other is even largely right. The internal administration of each seems to be impeccable but their diplomatic relations with one another seem to be internecine.

This whole set of lectures is intended to be an examination of a variety of concrete examples of dilemmas of this second kind.

But I shall adduce, here and now, three familiar examples in order to illustrate what I have so far described only in general terms.

The neuro-physiologist who is studying the mechanism of perception, like the physiologist who is studying the mechanism of digestion or reproduction, bases his theories upon the most solid kind of evidence that his work in the laboratory can provide, namely upon what he and his collaborators and assistants can see with the naked or the instrumentally assisted eye, and upon what they can hear, say, from the Geiger counter. Yet the theory of perception at which he arrives seems constitutionally to entail that there is an unbridgeable crevasse between what people, including himself, see or hear and what is really there—a crevasse so wide that he has apparently and can have no laboratory evidence that there exists even any correlation between what we perceive and what is really there. If his theory is true, then everyone is systematically debarred from perceiving the physical and physiological properties of things; and yet his theories are based on the very best experimental and observational evidence about the physical and physiological properties of such things as ear-drums and nerve-fibres. While at work in the laboratory he makes the best possible use of his eyes and ears; while writing up his results he has to deliver the severest possible censure upon these sham witnesses. He is sure that what they tell us can never be anything like the truth just because what they told him in his laboratory was of the highest reliability. From one point of view, which is that of laymen and scientists alike while actually exploring the world, we find out what is there by perceiving. From the other point of view, that of the inquirer into the mechanism of perception, what we perceive never coincides with what is in the world.

There are one or two features of this embarrassment which should be noticed. First, it is not a dispute between one physiologist and another. Doubtless there have been and are rival physiological hypotheses and theories, of which some will be defeated by others. But what are at loggerheads here are not two or more rival accounts of the mechanism of perception, but between a conclusion derivable apparently from *any* account of the mechanism of perception on the one side and everyone's workaday theory of perception on the other. Or, rather, I am stretching the word 'theory' over-violently when I say that the dispute is between a physiological theory of perception and another theory. For when we use our eyes and ears, whether in the garden or in the laboratory, we are not trading on any theory to the effect that we can find out the colours, shapes, positions and other characters of objects by seeing, hearing, tasting and the rest. We are finding out these things or else, sometimes, getting them wrong, but we are not doing so under instruction from any theory. We learn to use our eyes and tongues before we can consider the general question whether they are of any use; and we continue to use them without being influenced by the general doctrine that they are of some use or by the other general doctrine that they are of no use.

This point is sometimes expressed by saying that the conflict is one between a scientist's theory and a theory of Common Sense. But even this is misleading. It suggests, for one thing, that in using his eyes and ears the child is after all taking sides with a theory, only with a popular, amateurish and unformulated theory; and this is quite false. He is not considering any theoretical questions at all. It suggests for another thing that ability to find things out by seeing, hearing and the rest is dependent on, or is a part of, common sense, where this phrase has its usual connotation of a particular kind and degree of untutored judiciousness in coping with slightly out of the way, practical contingencies. I do not exhibit common sense or the lack of it in using a knife and fork. I do in dealing with a plausible beggar or with a mechanical breakdown when I have not got the proper tools.

Seemingly inescapable consequences of the physiologist's account of perception appear to demolish not just the credentials of some other theory of perception, but the credentials of perception itself; to cashier, that is, not just some supposed opinion held by all plain men about the reliability of their eyes and ears, but their eyes and ears themselves. This apparent conflict is not, then, to be described as a conflict between one theory and another theory, but rather as a conflict between a theory and a platitude; between what certain experts have thought out and what every one of us cannot but have learned by experience; between a doctrine and a piece of common knowledge.

Consider, next, a very different sort of dilemma. Everyone knows that unless a child is properly brought up he will probably not behave properly when grown up; and if he is properly brought up he is quite likely to behave properly when grown up. Everyone knows, too, that though certain actions of lunatics, epileptics, kleptomaniacs and drowning men are regrettable, they are not reprehensible or, of course, commendable either, where similar actions of a normal adult in normal situations are both regrettable and reprehensible. Yet if a person's bad conduct reflects his bad upbringing, it seems to follow that not he but his parents should be blamed—and then, of course, in their turn, his grandparents, his great-grandparents and in the end nobody at all. We feel quite sure both that a person can be made *moral* and that he cannot be *made* moral; and yet that both cannot be true. When considering the parents' duties, we have no doubt that they are to blame if they do not mould their son's conduct, feelings and thoughts. When considering the son's behaviour we have no doubt that he and not they should be blamed for some of the things that he does. Our answer to the one problem seems to rule out our answer to the other, and then at second remove to rule itself out too. We are embarrassed in partly similar ways if we substitute for his parents Heredity, Environment, Fate or God.

There is a feature of this embarrassment which is more strongly pronounced than was the case with the former dilemma about perception, namely that here it is very common for one and the same person to feel equally strong ties of allegiance to both of the seemingly discrepant positions. On Mondays, Wednesdays and Fridays he is sure that the will is free; on Tuesdays, Thursdays and Saturdays he is sure that causal explanations of actions can be found or are actually already known. Even if he does his best to forswear one view in favour of the other, his professions of conviction give forth a loud because hollow sound. In his heart he would prefer saying that he knows that both views are true to saying that he knows that actions have no causal explanations or that he knows that people are never to blame for what they do.

Another noteworthy feature of his embarrassment is this. Rival solutions of the same problem clamour for reinforcements.

The evidence or reasons for one hypothesis are palpably not yet strong enough if the evidence or reasons for its rivals still have some strength. If there remains anything to be said for them, not enough has yet been said for it. More evidence and better reasons must be found.

But in this logical dilemma which we are now considering and in all of the dilemmas which we shall be considering, each of the seemingly irreconcilable positions may have all the support that anyone could want for it. No one wants further evidence to be culled in favour of the proposition that well brought up children tend to behave better than badly brought up children; nor yet in favour of the proposition that some people sometimes behave reprehensibly. Certain sorts of theoretical disputes, such as those that we are to consider, are to be settled not by any internal corroboration of those positions, but by an arbitration of quite a different kind—not, for example, to put my cards on the table, by additional scientific researches, but by philosophical inquiries. Our concern is not with competitions but with litigations between lines of thought, where what is at stake is not which shall win and which shall lose a race, but what are their rights and obligations *vis à vis* one another and *vis à vis* also all other possible plaintiff and defendant positions.

In the two disputes that we have so far considered, the apparently warring theories or lines of thought were in a general way views about the same subject-matter, namely human conduct in the one case and perception in the other. But they were not rival solutions to the same question about that same subject-matter. The proposition that people tend to behave as they have been trained to behave is, perhaps, a somewhat truistic answer to the question 'What differences are made to a person by the scoldings and coaxings that he has received, the examples set to him, the advice, homilies and chastisements given to him, and so on?' But the proposition that some behaviour is reprehensible is a generalization of the answers to questions of the pattern 'Was he wrong to act as he did, or did he do it under duress or in an epileptic seizure?'

Similarly the proposition that we can discover some things by looking, others by listening, but none by dreaming, guessing, romancing or reminiscing is not an answer, true or false, to the question 'What is the mechanism of perception?' It is, rather, a platitudinous generalization of the answers to such questions as 'How did you find out that the clock had stopped?' or 'that the paint was wet?'

In a stretched sense of the word 'story', there can be two or twenty quite different sorts of stories about the same subject-matter, each of which may be supported by the best possible reasons for a story of that sort, and yet acceptance of one of these stories sometimes seems to require total rejection of at least one of the others as not merely a wrong story of its sort but as the wrong sort of story. Its credentials, however excellent of their kind, do it no good since they themselves are of a worthless kind.

I want now to illustrate this notion of litigation between theories or bodies of ideas with another well known example in order to bring out some other important points. In the eighteenth and again in the nineteenth century, the impressive advance of a science seemed to involve a corresponding retreat by religion. In turn mechanics, geology and biology were construed as challenges to religious belief. There was in progress, it was thought, a competition for a prize which would be lost by religion if it were won by science. We can see in retrospect that much of the impetus to philosophy in the first half of the eighteenth century and in the second half of the nineteenth century came from the seriousness of just these disputes.

The opening claims made were the simple ones. Theologians argued that there was no truth in Newton's physics or in Lyell's geology or in Darwin's biology. The champions of the new sciences correspondingly argued that there was no truth in theology. After a round or two both sides withdrew on certain points. Theologians ceased to defend Bishop Ussher's way of fixing the age of the earth, and admitted that, say, Lyell's way of fixing it was in principle the right way. Geological questions could not be answered from theological premisses. But conversely, pictures like the biologist T. H. Huxley's picture of man as a chess-player playing against an invisible opponent, came to be seen as a piece not of good scientific but of bad theological speculation. It had not a vestige of experimental backing. It was not a physical, a chemical or a biological hypothesis. In other ways it came off badly by comparison with the Christian picture.

It was not only baseless but also somewhat cheap, where the Christian picture, whatever its basis, not only was not cheap but itself taught the distinctions between what is cheap and what is precious. At the start the theologians had not had a suspicion that geological or biological questions were not continuous with theological questions; and many scientists had not come to suspect either that theological questions were not continuous with geological or biological questions. There was no visible or tangible fence between their questions. Expertness in one field was assumed to carry with it the techniques of handling problems in the other.

This instance shows not only how theorists of one kind may unwittingly commit themselves to propositions belonging to quite another province of thinking, but also how difficult it is for them, even after inter-theory litigation has begun, to realize just where the 'No Trespassing' notices should have been posted. In the country of concepts only a series of successful and unsuccessful prosecutions for trespass suffices to determine the boundaries and the rights of way.

There is another important point which is brought out by this historic but not yet archaic feud between theology and science. It would be a gross over-simplification, if a momentarily helpful one, to suppose that theology aims to provide the answer to just one question about the world, while geology, say, or biology aims to provide the answer to just one other, disparate, question about the world. Passport officials, perhaps, do try to get the answer to one question at a time and their questions are printed out for them on forms and are numbered off in serial order. But a theorist is not confronted by just one question, or even by a list of questions numbered off in serial order. He is faced by a tangle of wriggling, intertwined and slippery questions. Very often he has no clear idea what his questions are until he is well on the way towards answering them. He does not know, most of the time, even what is the general pattern of the theory that he is trying to construct, much less what are the precise forms and interconnexions of its ingredient questions. Often, as we shall see, he hopes and sometimes he is misled by the hope that the general pattern of his still rudimentary theory will be like that of some reputable theory which in another field has already reached completion or is near enough to completion for its logical architecture to be apparent. We, wise after the event, may say in retrospect 'Those litigating theorists ought to have seen that some of the propositions which they were championing and contesting belonged not to competing stories of the same general pattern but to non-competing stories of highly disparate patterns'. But how could they have seen this? Unlike playing-cards, problems and solutions of problems do not have their suits and their denominations printed on their faces. Only late in the game can the thinker know even what have been trumps.

Certainly there are some domains of thought between which inadvertent trespassing could not easily occur. The problems of the High Court Judge or the cryptographer are so well demarcated off from those of the chemist or the navigator that we should laugh at anyone who seriously pretended to settle juridical issues by electrolysis or to solve ciphers by radiolocation, as we do not laugh, straight off, at the programmes of 'evolutionary ethics' or 'psycho-analytic theology'. But even though we know quite well that radiolocation methods could not be applied to the cryptographer's problems, since his are not that sort of question, still we have no short or easy way of classifying into contrasted sorts the questions of cryptography and those of navigation. Cryptographers have questions not just of one kind but of multifarious kinds. So have navigators. Yet all or most crypto-graphic questions differ from all or most navigational questions so widely, not only in subject-matter but also in logical style, that we should have no reason for surprise if we found that a man, equally well trained in both disciplines, proved to be able to think powerfully and swiftly in the one field but only slowly and inefficiently in the other. A good High Court Judge might, in the same way, be an inferior thinker in matters of poker, algebra, finance or aerodynamics, however well coached he might be in its terminology and its techniques. The questions which belong to different domains of thought, differ very often not only in the kinds of subject-matter that they are about, but in the kinds of thinking that they require. So the segregation of questions into their kinds demands some very delicate discriminations of some very unpalpable features.

Part of the general point which I am trying to express is sometimes put by saying that the terms or concepts entering into the questions, statements and arguments of, say, the High Court Judge are of different 'categories' from those under which fall the terms or concepts of the chemist, the financier or the chess-player. So competing answers to the same question, though given in different terms, would still be in cognate terms of the same category or set of categories, whereas there could be no competition between answers to different questions, since the terms in which these very questions were posed would themselves be of alien categories. This idiom can be helpful as a familiar mnemonic with some beneficial associations. It can also be an impediment, if credited with the virtues of a skeleton-key. I think it is worth while to take some pains with this word 'category', but not for the usual reason, namely that there exists an exact, professional way of using it, in which, like a skeleton-key, it will turn all our locks for us; but rather for the unusual reason that there is an inexact, amateurish way of using it in which, like a coal-hammer, it will make a satisfactory knocking noise on doors which we want opened to us. It gives the answers to none of our questions but it can be made to arouse people to the questions in a properly brusque way.

Aristotle for some excellent purposes of his own worked out an inventory of some ten heads of elementary questions that can be asked about an individual thing or person. We can ask of what sort it is, what it is like, how tall, wide or heavy it is, where it is, what are its dates, what it is doing, what is being done to it, in what condition it is and one or two others. To each such question there corresponds a range of possible answering-terms, one of which will, in general, be true and the rest false of the individual concerned. The terms satisfying one such interrogative will not be answers, true or false, to any of the other interrogatives. '158 pounds' does not inform you or misinform you about what Socrates is doing, where he is or what sort of a creature he is. Terms satisfying the same interrogative are then said to be of the same category; terms satisfying different interrogatives are of different categories.

Now, aside from the fact that Aristotle's inventory of possible interrogatives about an individual may contain redundancies and certainly is capable of indefinite expansion, we have to notice the much more important fact that only a vanishingly small fraction of askable questions are demands for information about designated individuals. What questions, for example, are asked by economists, statisticians, mathematicians, philosophers or grammarians which would be answered, truly or falsely, by statements of the pattern 'He is a cannibal' or 'It is now simmering'?

Some loyal Aristotelians, who like all loyalists ossified their master's teaching, treated his list of categories as providing the pigeon-holes in one or other of which there could and should be lodged every term used or usable in technical or untechnical discourse. Every concept must be either of Category I or of Category II or... of Category X. Even in our own day there exist thinkers who, so far from finding this supply of pigeonholes intolerably exiguous, find it gratuitously lavish; and are prepared to say of any concept presented to them 'Is it a Quality? If not, then it must be a Relation'. In opposition to such views, it should suffice to launch this challenge: 'In which of your two or ten pigeon-holes will you lodge the following six terms, drawn pretty randomly from the glossary of Contract Bridge alone, namely "singleton", "trump", "vulnerable", "slam", "finesse" and "revoke"?' The vocabularies of the law, of physics, of theology and of musical criticism are not poorer than that of Bridge. The truth is that there are not just two or just ten different logical *métiers* open to the terms or concepts we employ in ordinary and technical discourse, there are indefinitely many such different *métiers* and indefinitely many dimensions of these differences.

I adduced the six Bridge terms, 'singleton', 'trump', 'vulnerable', 'slam', 'finesse' and 'revoke', as terms none of which will go into any one of Aristotle's ten pigeon-holes. But now we should notice as well that, though all alike belong to the specialist lingo of a single card-game, not one of them is, in an enlarged sense of 'category', of the same category with any of the other five. We can ask whether a card is a diamond or a spade or a club or a heart; but not whether a card is a singleton or a trump; not whether a game ended in a slam or in a revoke; not whether a pair of players is vulnerable or a finesse. None of the terms is a co-member of an either–or set with any of the others. The same thing is true of most though naturally not of all of the terms that one might pick at random out of the glossaries of financiers, ecologists, surgeons, garage-mechanics and legislators.

It follows directly that neither the propositions which embody such concepts nor the questions which would be answered, truly or falsely, by such propositions admit of being automatically entered into a ready-made register of logical kinds or types. Where we can fairly easily and promptly docket short, specimen sentences as being of this or that registered grammatical pattern, we have no corresponding register of logical patterns, direct reference to which enables us without more ado to accomplish the logical parsing of propositions and questions. A logician, however acute, who does not know the game of Bridge, cannot by simple inspection find out what is and what is not implied by the statement 'North has revoked'. For all he can tell by simple inspection, the statement may be giving information of the same quality as that given by the statement 'North has coughed'.

To pull some threads together. Sometimes thinkers are at loggerheads with one another, not because their propositions do conflict, but because their authors fancy that they conflict. They suppose themselves to be giving, at least by indirect implication, rival answers to the same questions, when this is not really the case. They are then talking at cross-purposes with one another. It can be convenient to characterize these cross-purposes by saying that the two sides are, at certain points, hinging their arguments upon concepts of different categories, though they suppose themselves to be hinging them upon different concepts of the same category, or vice versa. But it is not more than convenient. It still remains to be shown that the discrepancies are discrepancies of this general kind, and this can be done only by showing in detail how the *métiers* in ratiocination of the concepts under pressure are more dissimilar from one another or less dissimilar from one another than the contestants had unwittingly supposed.

My object in the following pages is to examine a number of specimens of what I construe as litigations and not mere competitions between theories or lines of thought, and to bring out both what seems to be at stake in those disputes and what is really at stake. I shall also try to exhibit what sorts of considerations can and should settle the real claims and counter-claims.

But I have one apology to offer for this programme and one *démenti* to make about it. Mr Tarner who endowed these lectures wished the lecturers to discuss 'the Philosophy of the Sciences and the Relations or Want of Relations between the different Departments of Knowledge'. He hoped, I gather, that it would be to the Want of Relations that we should chiefly testify—a piece of unsentimentalism which I find pleasingly astringent.

Now I should probably have complied most faithfully with Mr Tarner's wishes had I, like most of my predecessors, chosen to discuss certain of the disputes in which are involved two or more of the accredited sciences. I have heard rumours, for example, of sovereignty-disputes between the physical and the biological sciences and of boundary-disputes between psychologists and Judges. But I am disqualified from trying to arbitrate in these disputes by the simple bar of technical ignorance. I have no first-hand and very little second-hand knowledge of the specialized ideas between which these systems of thought are braced. I have long since learned to doubt the native sagacity of philosophers when discussing technicalities which they have not learned to handle on the job, as in earlier days I learned to doubt the judgements of those towing-path critics who had never done any rowing. Arbitrators should certainly be neutral, but they should also know from inside what the disputants are so hotly fighting on behalf of and against.

However, I am not very contrite about these disabilities of mine. For one thing, the theoretical dilemmas which I shall examine are likely to resemble in some important respects some of the more esoteric dilemmas which I must pass by. If I can throw any light on the matters which I shall discuss, some of this light may be reflected on to matters upon which I shall be silent. For another and more important thing, I suspect that the most radical cross-purposes between specialist theories derive from the logical trickiness not of the highly technical concepts employed in them, but of the underlying non-technical concepts employed as well in them as in everyone else's thinking.

Different travellers use vehicles of highly intricate constructions and of very different makes for all the varying purposes of their very dissimilar journeys, and yet are alike in using the same public roads and the same signposts as one another. Somewhat so, thinkers may use all sorts of specially designed concepts for their several purposes, but still have also to use the same highway concepts. Usually, too, the traveller's doubts and mistakes about his bearings arise, not because anything in his private vehicle behaves awkwardly, but because the public road is a tricky road. The ways in which it tricks the driver of the limousine are just the same as the ways in which it tricks the humble cyclist or pedestrian.

The *démenti* which I wish to make about my programme is this. I have said that when intellectual positions are at cross-purposes in the manner which I have sketchily described and illustrated, the solution of their quarrel cannot come from any further internal corroboration of either position. The kind of thinking which advances biology is not the kind of thinking which settles the claims and counter-claims between biology and physics. These inter-theory questions are not questions internal to those theories. They are not biological or physical questions. They are philosophical questions.

Now I daresay that my title has aroused the expectation, perhaps the hope, perhaps the fear, that I should be discussing some of the disputes that have arisen between one philosophical school and another philosophical school—the feud, for example, between Idealists and Realists, or the vendetta between Empiricists and Rationalists. But I shall not try to interest you in these domestic differences. I am not interested in them myself. They do not matter.

But in saying that these much advertised differences do not matter, I do not mean that all philosophers really see eye to eye. It would, I am glad to say, be nearer the truth to say that they seldom see eye to eye if they are any good and if they are discussing live issues and not dead ones. A live issue is a piece of country in which no one knows which way to go. As there are no paths, there are no paths to share. Where there are paths to share, there are paths; and paths are the memorials of undergrowth already cleared.

None the less, though philosophers are and ought to be highly critical persons, their wrangles are not the by-products of loyalty to a party or a school of thought. There do, of course, exist in our midst and inside our skins plenty of disciples, heresy-hunters and electioneers; only these are not philosophers but something else that goes by the same long-suffering name. Karl Marx was sapient enough to deny the impeachment that he was a Marxist. So too Plato was, in my view, a very unreliable Platonist. He was too much of a philosopher to think that anything that he had said was the last word. It was left to his disciples to identify his footmarks with his destination.

II

'IT WAS TO BE'

I WANT now to launch out without more ado into the full presentation and discussion of a concrete dilemma. It is a dilemma
which, I expect, has occasionally bothered all of us, though, in
its simplest form, not very often or for very long at a time. But
it is intertwined with two other dilemmas, both of which probably have seriously worried nearly all of us. In its pure form it
has not been seriously canvassed by any important Western
philosopher, though the Stoics drew on it at certain points. It
was, however, an ingredient in discussions of the theological
doctrine of Predestination and I suspect that it has exerted a
surreptitious influence on some of the champions and opponents
of Determinism.

At a certain moment yesterday evening I coughed and at a
certain moment yesterday evening I went to bed. It was therefore true on Saturday that on Sunday I would cough at the one
moment and go to bed at the other. Indeed, it was true a
thousand years ago that at certain moments on a certain Sunday
a thousand years later I should cough and go to bed. But if it was
true beforehand—forever beforehand—that I was to cough and
go to bed at those two moments on Sunday, 25 January 1953,
then it was impossible for me not to do so. There would be a
contradiction in the joint assertion that it was true that I would
do something at a certain time and that I did not do it. This
argument is perfectly general. Whatever anyone ever does, whatever happens anywhere to anything, could not *not* be done or
happen, if it was true beforehand that it was going to be done or
was going to happen. So everything, including everything that
we do, has been definitively booked from any earlier date you
like to choose. Whatever is, was to be. So nothing that does
occur could have been helped and nothing that has not actually
been done could possibly have been done.

This point, that for whatever takes place it was antecedently
true that it was going to take place, is sometimes picturesquely
expressed by saying that the Book of Destiny has been written

up in full from the beginning of time. A thing's actually taking place is, so to speak, merely the turning up of a passage that has for all time been written. This picture has led some fatalists to suppose that God, if there is one, or, we ourselves, if suitably favoured, may have access to this book and read ahead. But this is a fanciful embellishment upon what in itself is a severe and seemingly rigorous argument. We may call it 'the fatalist argument'.

Now the conclusion of this argument from antecedent truth, namely that nothing can be helped, goes directly counter to the piece of common knowledge that some things are our own fault, that some threatening disasters can be foreseen and averted, and that there is plenty of room for precautions, planning and weighing alternatives. Even when we say nowadays of someone that he is born to be hanged or not born to be drowned, we say it as a humorous archaism. We really think that it depends very much on himself whether he is hanged or not, and that his chances of drowning are greater if he refuses to learn to swim. Yet even we are not altogether proof against the fatalist view of things. In a battle I may well come to the half-belief that either there exists somewhere behind the enemy lines a bullet with my name on it, or there does not, so that taking cover is either of no avail or else unnecessary. In card-games and at the roulette-table it is easy to subside into the frame of mind of fancying that our fortunes are in some way prearranged, well though we know that it is silly to fancy this.

But how can we deny that whatever happens was booked to happen from all eternity? What is wrong with the argument from antecedent truth to the inevitability of what the antecedent truths are antecedently true about? For it certainly is logically impossible for a prophecy to be true and yet the event prophesied not to come about.

We should notice first of all that the premiss of the argument does not require that anyone, even God, *knows* any of these antecedent truths, or to put it picturesquely, that the Book of Destiny has been written by anybody or could be perused by anybody. This is just what distinguishes the pure fatalist argument from the mixed theological argument for predestination. This latter argument does turn on the supposition that God at least has foreknowledge of what is to take place, and perhaps also pre-ordains it. But the pure fatalist argument turns only on the principle that it was true that a given thing would happen, before it did happen, i.e. that what is, was to be; not that it was known by anyone that it was to be. Yet even when we try hard to bear this point in mind, it is very easy inadvertently to reinterpret this initial principle into the supposition that before the thing happened it was known by someone that it was booked to happen. For there is something intolerably vacuous in the idea of the eternal but unsupported pre-existence of truths in the future tense. When we say 'a thousand years ago it was true that I should now be saying what I am', it is so difficult to give any body to this 'it' of which we say that it was then true, that we unwittingly fill it out with the familiar body of an expectation which someone once entertained, or of a piece of foreknowledge which someone once possessed. Yet to do this is to convert a principle which was worrying because, in a way, totally truistic, into a supposition which is unworrying because quasi-historical, entirely without evidence and most likely just false.

Very often, though certainly not always, when we say 'it was true that...' or 'it is false that...' we are commenting on some actual pronouncement made or opinion held by some identifiable person. Sometimes we are commenting in a more general way on a thing which some people, unidentified and perhaps un-identifiable, have believed or now believe. We can comment on the belief in the Evil Eye without being able to name anyone who held it; we know that plenty of people did hold it. Thus we can say 'it was true' or 'it is false' in passing verdicts upon the pronouncements both of named and of nameless authors. But in the premiss of the fatalist argument, namely that it was true before something happened that it would happen, there is no implication of anyone, named or unnamed, having made that prediction.

There remains a third thing that might be meant by 'it was true a thousand years ago that a thousand years later these things would be being said in this place', namely that *if* anybody had made a prediction to this effect, though doubtless nobody did, he would have been right. It is not a case of an actual pre-diction having come true but of a conceivable prediction having come true. The event has not made an actual prophecy come true. It has made a might-have-been prophecy come true.

Or can we say even this? A target can be hit by an actual bullet, but can it be hit by a might-have-been bullet? Or should we rather say only that it could have been hit by a might-have-been bullet? The historical-sounding phrases 'came true', 'made true' and 'was fulfilled' apply well enough to predictions actually made, but there is a detectable twist, which may be an illegitimate twist, in saying that a might-have-been prediction did come true or was made true by the event. If an unbacked horse wins a race, we can say that it would have won money for its backers, if only there had been any. But we cannot say that it did win money for its backers, if only there had been any. There is no answer to the question 'How much money did it win for them?' Correspondingly, we cannot with a clear conscience say of an event that it has fulfilled the predictions of it which could have been made, but only that it would have fulfilled any predictions of it which might have been made. There is no answer to the question 'Within what limits of precision were these might-have-been predictions correct about the time and the loudness of my cough?'

Let us consider the notions of truth and falsity. In characterizing somebody's statement, for example a statement in the future tense, as true or as false, we usually though not always, mean to convey rather more than that what was forecast did or did not take place. There is something of a slur in 'false' and something honorific in 'true', some suggestion of the insincerity or sincerity of its author, or some suggestion of his rashness or cautiousness as an investigator. This is brought out by our reluctance to characterize either as true or as false pure and avowed guesses. If you make a guess at the winner of the race, it will turn out right or wrong, correct or incorrect, but hardly true or false. These epithets are inappropriate to avowed guesses, since the one epithet pays an extra tribute, the other conveys an extra adverse criticism of the maker of the guess, neither of which can he merit. In guessing there is no place for sincerity or insincerity, or for caution or rashness in investigation. To make a guess is not to give an assurance and it is not to declare the result of an investigation. Guessers are neither reliable nor unreliable.

Doubtless we sometimes use 'true' without intending any connotation of trustworthiness and, much less often, 'false' without any connotation of trust misplaced. But, for safety's sake, let us reword the fatalist argument in terms of these thinner words, 'correct' and 'incorrect'. It would now run as follows. For any event that takes place, an antecedent guess, if anyone had made one, that it was going to take place, would have been correct, and an antecedent guess to the contrary, if anyone had made it, would have been incorrect. This formulation already sounds less alarming than the original formulation. The word 'guess' cuts out the covert threat of foreknowledge, or of there being budgets of antecedent forecasts, all meriting confidence before the event. What, now, of the notion of guesses in the future tense being correct or incorrect?

Antecedently to the running of most horse-races, some people guess that one horse will win, some that another will. Very often every horse has its backers. If, then, the race is run and won, then some of the backers will have guessed correctly and the rest will have guessed incorrectly. To say that someone's guess that Eclipse would win was correct is to say no more than that he guessed that Eclipse would win and Eclipse did win. But can we say in retrospect that his guess, which he made before the race, was already correct before the race? He made the correct guess two days ago, but was his guess correct during those two days? It certainly was not incorrect during those two days, but it does not follow, though it might seem to follow, that it was correct during those two days. Perhaps we feel unsure which we ought to say, whether that his guess was correct during those two days, though no one could know it to be so, or only that, as it turned out, it was during those two days going to prove correct, i.e. that the victory which did, in the event, make it correct had not yet happened. A prophecy is not fulfilled until the event forecast has happened. Just here is where 'correct' resembles 'fulfilled' and differs importantly from 'true'. The honorific connotations of 'true' can certainly attach to a person's forecasts from the moment at which they are made, so that if these forecasts turn out incorrect, while we withdraw the word 'true', we do not necessarily withdraw the testimonials which it carried. The establishment of incorrectness certainly cancels 'true' but not, as a rule, so fiercely as to incline us to say 'false'.

The words 'true' and 'false' and the words 'correct' and 'incorrect' are adjectives, and this grammatical fact tempts us to suppose that trueness and falseness, correctness and incorrectness, and even, perhaps, fulfilledness and unfulfilledness must be qualities or properties resident in the propositions which they characterize. As sugar is sweet and white from the moment it comes into existence to the moment when it goes out of existence, so we are tempted to infer, by parity of reasoning, that the trueness or correctness of predictions and guesses must be features or properties which belong all the time to their possessors, whether we can detect their presence in them or not. But if we consider that 'deceased', 'lamented' and 'extinct' are also adjectives, and yet certainly do not apply to people or mastodons while they exist, but only after they have ceased to exist, we may feel more cordial towards the idea that 'correct' is in a partly similar way a merely obituary and valedictory epithet, as 'fulfilled' more patently is. It is more like a verdict than a description. So when I tell you that if anyone had guessed that Eclipse would win today's race his guess would have turned out correct, I give you no more information about the past than is given by the evening newspaper which tells you that Eclipse won the race.

I want now to turn to the fatalist conclusion, namely that since whatever is was to be, therefore nothing can be helped. The argument seems to compel us to say that since the antecedent truth requires the event of which it is the true forecast, therefore this event is in some disastrous way fettered to or driven by or bequeathed by that antecedent truth—as if my coughing last night was made or obliged to occur by the antecedent truth that it was going to occur, perhaps in something like the way in which gunfire makes the windows rattle a moment or two after the discharge. What sort of necessity would this be?

To bring this out let us by way of contrast suppose that someone produced the strictly parallel argument, that for everything that happens, it is true for ever *afterwards* that it happened.

I coughed last night, so it is true today and will be true a thousand years hence that I coughed last night. But these posterior truths in the past tense, could not be true without my having coughed. Therefore my coughing was necessitated or obliged to have happened by the truth of these posterior chronicles of it. Clearly something which disturbed us in the original form of the argument is missing in this new form. We cheerfully grant that the occurrence of an event involves and is involved by the truth of subsequent records, actual or conceivable, to the effect that it occurred. For it does not even seem to render the occurrence a product or effect of these truths about it. On the contrary, in this case we are quite clear that it is the occurrence which makes the posterior truths about it true, not the posterior truths which make the occurrence occur. These posterior truths are shadows cast by the events, not the events shadows cast by these truths about them, since these belong to the posterity, not to the ancestry of the events.

Why does the fact that a posterior truth about an occurrence requires that occurrence not worry us in the way in which the fact that an anterior truth about an occurrence requires that occurrence does worry us? Why does the slogan 'Whatever is, always was to be' seem to imply that nothing can be helped, where the obverse slogan 'Whatever is, will always have been' does not seem to imply this? We are not exercised by the notorious fact that when the horse has already escaped it is too late to shut the stable door. We are sometimes exercised by the idea that as the horse is either going to escape or not going to escape, to shut the stable door beforehand is either unavailing or unnecessary. A large part of the reason is that in thinking of a predecessor making its successor necessary we unwittingly assimilate the necessitation to causal necessitation. Gunfire makes windows rattle a few seconds later, but rattling windows do not make gunfire happen a few seconds earlier, even though they may be perfect evidence that gunfire did happen a few seconds earlier. We slide, that is, into thinking of the anterior truths as *causes* of the happenings about which they were true, where the mere matter of their relative dates saves us from thinking of happenings as the effects of those truths about them which are posterior to them. Events cannot be the effects of their successors, any more than we can be the offspring of our posterity.

So let us look more suspiciously at the notions of *necessitating*, *making*, *obliging*, *requiring* and *involving* on which the argument turns. How is the notion of *requiring* or *involving* that we have been working with related to the notion of *causing*?

It is quite true that a backer cannot guess correctly that Eclipse will win without Eclipse winning and still it is quite false that his guessing made or caused Eclipse to win. To say that his guess that Eclipse would win was correct does logically involve or require that Eclipse won. To assert the one and deny the other would be to contradict oneself. To say that the backer guessed correctly is just to say that the horse which he guessed would win, did win. The one assertion cannot be true without the other assertion being true. But in this way in which one truth may require or involve another truth, an event cannot be one of the implications of a truth. Events can be effects, but they cannot be implications. Truths can be consequences of other truths, but they cannot be causes of effects or effects of causes.

In much the same way, the truth that someone revoked involves the truth that he had in his hand at least one card of the suit led. But he was not forced or coerced into having a card of that suit in his hand by the fact that he revoked. He could not both have revoked and not had a card of that suit in his hand, but this 'could not' does not connote any kind of duress. A proposition can imply another proposition, but it cannot thrust a card into a player's hand. The questions, what makes things happen, what prevents them from happening, and whether we can help them or not, are entirely unaffected by the logical truism that a statement to the effect that something happens, is correct if and only if it happens. Lots of things could have prevented Eclipse from winning the race; lots of other things could have made his lead a longer one. But one thing had no influence on the race at all, namely the fact that if anyone guessed that he would win, he guessed correctly.

We are now in a position to separate out one unquestionable and very dull true proposition from another exciting but entirely false proposition, both of which seem to be conveyed by the slogan 'What is, always was to be'. It is an unquestionable and very dull truth that for anything that happens, if anyone had at any previous time made the guess that it would happen, his guess would have turned out correct. The twin facts that the event could not take place without such a guess turning out correct and that such a guess could not turn out correct without the event taking place tell us nothing whatsoever about how the event was caused, whether it could have been prevented, or even whether it could have been predicted with certainty or probability from what had happened before. The menacing statement that what is was to be, construed in one way, tells us only the trite truth that if it is true to say (*a*) that something happened, then it is also true to say (*b*) that that original statement (*a*) is true, no matter when this latter comment (*b*) on the former statement (*a*) may be made.

The exciting but false proposition that the slogan seems to force upon us is that whatever happens is inevitable or doomed, and, what makes it sound even worse, *logically* inevitable or *logically* doomed—somewhat as it is logically inevitable that the immediate successor of any even number is an odd number. So what does 'inevitable' mean? An avalanche may be, for all practical purposes, unavoidable. A mountaineer in the direct path of an avalanche can himself do nothing to stop the avalanche or get himself out of its way, though a providential earthquake might conceivably divert the avalanche or a helicopter might conceivably lift him out of danger. His position is much worse, but only much worse, than that of a cyclist half a mile ahead of a lumbering steam-roller. It is extremely unlikely that the steam-roller will catch up with him at all, and even if it does so it is extremely likely that its driver will halt or that the cyclist himself will move off in good time. But these differences between the plights of the mountaineer and the cyclist are differences of degree only. The avalanche is practically unavoidable, but it is not logically inevitable. Only conclusions can be logically inevitable, given the premises, and an avalanche is not a conclusion. The fatalist doctrine, by contrast, is that everything is absolutely and logically inevitable in a way in which the avalanche is not absolutely or logically inevitable; that we are all absolutely and logically powerless where even the hapless mountaineer is only in a desperate plight and the cyclist is in no real danger at all; that everything is fettered by the Law of Contradiction to taking the course it does take, as odd numbers are bound to succeed even numbers. What sort of fetters are these purely logical fetters?

Certainly there are infinitely many cases of one truth making necessary the truth of another proposition. The truth that today is Monday makes necessary the truth of the proposition that tomorrow is Tuesday. It cannot be Monday today without tomorrow being Tuesday. A person who said 'It is Monday today but not Tuesday tomorrow' would be taking away with his left hand what he was giving with his right hand. But in the way in which some truths carry other truths with them or make them necessary, events themselves cannot be made necessary by truths. Things and events may be the topics of premises and conclusions, but they cannot themselves be premises or conclusions. You may preface a statement by the word 'therefore', but you cannot pin either a 'therefore' or a 'perhaps not' on to a person or an avalanche. It is a partial parallel to say that while a sentence may contain or may be without a split infinitive, a road accident cannot either contain or lack a split infinitive, even though it is what a lot of sentences, with or without split infinitives in them, are about. It is true that an avalanche may be practically inescapable and the conclusion of an argument may be logically inescapable, but the avalanche has not got—nor does it lack—the inescapability of the conclusion of an argument. The fatalist theory tries to endue happenings with the inescapability of the conclusions of valid arguments. Our familiarity with the practical inescapability of some things, like some avalanches, helps us to yield to the view that really everything that happens is inescapable, only not now in the way in which some avalanches are inescapable and others not, but in the way in which logical consequences are inescapable, given their premises. The fatalist has tried to characterize happenings by predicates which are proper only to conclusions of arguments. He tried to flag my cough with a Q.E.D.

Before standing back to draw some morals from this dilemma between *whatever is was to be* and *some things which have happened could have been averted*, I want briefly to discuss one further point which may be of only domestic interest to professional philosophers. If a city-engineer has constructed a roundabout where there had been dangerous cross-roads, he may properly claim to have reduced the number of accidents. He may say that lots of accidents that would otherwise have occurred have been prevented by his piece of road improvement. But suppose we now ask him to give us a list of the particular accidents which he has averted. He can do nothing but laugh at us. If an accident has not happened, there is no 'it' to put down on a list of 'accidents prevented'. He can say that accidents of such and such kinds which used to be frequent are now rare. But he cannot say 'Yesterday's collision at midday between this fire-engine and that milk-float at this corner was, fortunately, averted'. There was no such collision, so he cannot say '*This* collision was averted'. To generalize this, we can never point to or name a particular happening and say of it 'This happening was averted', and this logical truism seems to commit us to saying 'No happenings can be averted' and consequently 'it's no good trying to ensure or prevent anything happening'. So when we try to say that some things that happen could have been prevented; that some drownings, for example, would not have occurred had their victims learned to swim, we seem to be in a queer logical fix. We can say that a particular person would not have drowned had he been able to swim. But we cannot quite say that his lamented drowning would have been averted by swimming-lessons. For had he taken those lessons, he would not have drowned, and then we would not have had for a topic of discussion just that lamented drowning of which we want to say that *it* would have been prevented. We are left bereft of any 'it' at all. Averted fatalities are not fatalities. In short, we cannot, in logic, say of any designated fatality that it was averted—and this sounds like saying that it is logically impossible to avert any fatalities.

The situation is parallel to the following. If my parents had never met, I should not have been born, and had Napoleon known some things that he did not know the Battle of Waterloo would not have been fought. So we want to say that certain contingencies would have prevented me from being born and the Battle of Waterloo from being fought. But then there would have been no Gilbert Ryle and no Battle of Waterloo for historians to describe as not having been born and as not having been fought. What does not exist or happen cannot be named, individually indicated or put on a list, and cannot therefore be characterized as having been prevented from existing or happening. So though we are right to say that some sorts of accidents can be prevented, we cannot put this by saying that this designated accident might have been prevented from occurring —not because it was of an unpreventable sort, but because neither 'preventable' nor 'unpreventable' can be epithets of designated occurrences, any more than 'exists' or 'does not exist' can be predicated of designated things or persons. As 'unborn' cannot without absurdity be an epithet of a named person, so 'born' cannot without a queerly penetrating sort of redundancy be an epithet of him either. The question 'Were you born or not?' is, unless special insurance-policies are taken out, an unaskable question. Who could be asked it? Nor could one ask whether the Battle of Waterloo was fought or unfought. That it was fought goes with our having an *it* to talk about at all. There could not be a list of unfought battles, and a list of fought battles would contain just what a list of battles would contain. The question 'Could the Battle of Waterloo have been unfought?', taken in one way, is an absurd question. Yet its absurdity is something quite different from the falsity that Napoleon's strategic decisions were forced upon him by the laws of logic.

I suspect that some of us have felt that the fatalist doctrine is unrefuted so long as no remedy has been found for the smell of logical trickiness that hangs about such arguments as 'Accidents can be prevented; therefore *this* accident could have been prevented' or 'I can bottle up my laughter; therefore I could have bottled up *that* hoot of laughter'. For it would not have been a hoot at all, and so not *that* hoot, had I bottled up my laughter. I could not, logically, have bottled *it* up. For *it* was an unbottled up hoot of laughter. The fact that it occurred is already contained in my allusion to 'that hoot of laughter'. So a sort of contradiction is produced when I try to say that that hoot of laughter need not have occurred. No such contradiction is produced when I say 'I did not have to hoot with laughter'. It is the demonstrative word '*that*...' which refused to consort with '...did not occur' or '...might not have occurred'.

This point seems to me to bring out an important difference between anterior truths and posterior truths, or between prophecies and chronicles. After 1815 there could be true and false statements mentioning the Battle of Waterloo in the past tense. After 1900 there could be true and false statements in the present and past tenses mentioning me. But before 1815 and 1900 there could not be true or false statements giving individual mention to the Battle of Waterloo or to me, and this not just because our names had not yet been given, nor yet just because no one happened to be well enough equipped to predict the future in very great detail, but for some more abstruse reason. The prediction of an event can, in principle, be as specific as you please. It does not matter if in fact no forecaster could know or reasonably believe his prediction to be true. If gifted with a lively imagination, he could freely concoct a story in the future tense with all sorts of minutiae in it and this elaborate story might happen to come true. But one thing he could not do—logically and not merely epistemologically could not do. He could not get the future events themselves for the heroes or heroines of his story, since while it is still an askable question whether or not a battle will be fought at Waterloo in 1815, he cannot use with their normal force the phrase 'the Battle of Waterloo' or the pronoun 'it'. While it is still an askable question whether my parents are going to have a fourth son, he cannot use as a name the name 'Gilbert Ryle' or use as a pronoun designating their fourth son the pronoun 'he'. Roughly, statements in the future tense cannot convey singular, but only general propositions, where statements in the present and past tense can convey both. More strictly, a statement to the effect that something will exist or happen is, in *so far*, a general statement. When I predict the next eclipse of the moon, I have indeed got the moon to make statements about, but I have not got her next eclipse to make statements about. Perhaps this is why novelists never write in the future tense, but only in the past tense. They could not get even the semblances of heroes or heroines into prophetic fiction, since the future tense of their would-be-prophetic mock-narratives would leave it open for their heroes and heroines not to be born. But as my phrase 'I have not got it to make statements about' stirs up a nest of logical hornets, I shall bid farewell for the present to this matter.

I have chosen to start with this particular dilemma for

moderately sustained discussion for two or three connected reasons. But I did not do so for the reason that the issue is or ever has been of paramount importance in the Western world. No philosopher of the first or second rank has defended fatalism or been at great pains to attack it. Neither religion nor science wants it. Right-wing and Left-wing doctrines borrow nothing from it. On the other hand we do all have our fatalist moments; we do all know from inside what it is like to regard the course of events as the continuous unrolling of a scroll written from the beginning of time and admitting of no additions or amendments. Yet though we know what it is like to entertain this idea, still we are unimpassioned about it. We are not secret zealots for it or secret zealots against it. We are, nearly all of the time, though also aware that the argument for them is hard to rebut, cheerfully sure that the fatalist conclusions are false. The result is that we can study the issue in the spirit of critical playgoers, not that of electors whose votes are being solicited. It is not a burning issue. This is one reason why I have started with it.

Next, so little has the issue been debated by Western thinkers that I have been free to formulate for myself not only what seem to me the false steps in the fatalist argument from antecedent truth, but even that argument itself. I have not had to recapitulate a traditional controversy between philosophical schools, since there has been next to no such controversy, as there have, notoriously, existed protracted controversies about Predestination and Determinism. You know, from inside your own skins, all that needs to be known about the issue. There are no cards of erudition up my sleeve.

Thirdly, the issue is in a way a very simple one, a very important one and an illuminatingly tricky one. It is simple in that so few pivot-concepts are involved—just, in the first instance, the untechnical concepts of *event, before* and *after, truth, necessity, cause, prevention, fault* and *responsibility*—and of course we all know our ways about in them—or do we? They are public highway concepts, not craftsmen's concepts; so none of us can get lost in them—or can we? It is important in that if the fatalist conclusion were true, then nearly the whole of our normal religious, moral, political, historical, scientific and pedagogic thinking would be on entirely the wrong lines. We cannot shape the world of tomorrow, since it has already been shaped once and for all. It is a tricky issue because there is not any regulation or argumentative manœuvre by which it can be settled. I have produced quite an apparatus of somewhat elaborate arguments, all of which need expansion and reinforcement. I expect that the logical ice is pretty thin under some of them. It would not trouble me if the ice broke, since the stamp of the foot which broke it would itself be a partially decisive move. But even this move would not be the playing of any regulation logical manœuvre. Such regulation manœuvres exist only for dead philosophical issues. It was their death which promoted the decisive moves up to the status of regulation manœuvres.

Now for some general morals which can be drawn from the existence of this dilemma and from attempts to resolve it. It arose out of two seemingly innocent and unquestionable propositions, propositions which are so well embedded in what I may vaguely call 'common knowledge' that we should hardly wish to give them the grand title of 'theories'. These two propositions were, first, that some statements in the future tense are or come true, and, second, that we often can and sometimes should secure that certain things do happen and that certain other things do not happen. Neither of these innocent-seeming propositions is as yet a philosopher's speculation, or even a scientist's hypothesis or a theologian's doctrine. They are just platitudes. We should, however, notice that it would not very often occur to anyone to state these platitudes. People say of this particular prediction that it was fulfilled and of that particular guess that it turned out correct. To say that some statements in the future tense are true is a generalization of these particular concrete comments. But it is a generalization which there is not usually any point in propounding. Similarly people say of particular offences that they ought not to have been committed and of particular catastrophes that they could or could not have been prevented. It is relatively rare to stand back and say in general terms that people sometimes do wrong and that mishaps are sometimes our own fault. None the less, there are occasions, long before philosophical or scientific speculations begin, on which people do deliver generalities of these sorts. It is part of the business of the teacher and the preacher, of the judge and the

doctor, of Solon and Æsop, to say general things, with concrete
examples of which everyone is entirely familiar. In one way the
generality is not and cannot be news to anyone that every day has
its yesterday and every day has its tomorrow; and yet, in another
way, this can be a sort of news. There was the first occasion on
which this generality was presented to us, and very surprising it
was—despite the fact that on every day since infancy we had
thought about its particular yesterday and its particular tomorrow. There is, anyhow at the start, an important sort of
unfamiliarity about such generalizations of the totally familiar.
We do not yet know how we should and how we should not
operate with them, although we know quite well how to operate
with the daily particularities of which they are the generalizations. We make no foot-faults on Monday morning with 'will be'
and 'was'; but when required to deal in the general case with
the notions of *the future* and *the past*, we are no longer sure of
our feet.

The two platitudes from which the trouble arose are not in
direct conflict with one another. It is real or seeming deductions
from the one which quarrel with the other, or else with real or
seeming deductions from it. They are not rivals such that before
these deductions had been noticed anyone would want to say
'I accept the proposition that some statements in the future
tense are fulfilled, so naturally I reject the proposition that some
things need not and should not have happened'. It is because
the former proposition seems indirectly to entail that what
was from all eternity going to be and because this, in its turn,
seems to entail that nothing is anybody's fault, that some
thinkers have felt forced to make a choice between the two
platitudes. Aristotle, for example, rejected, with reservations,
the platitude that statements in the future tense are true or false.
Certain Stoics rejected the platitude that we are responsible for
some things that happen. If we accept both platitudes, it is
because we think that the fatalist deductions from 'it was
true...' are fallacious or else that certain deductions drawn
from 'some things are our fault' are fallacious, or both.

But this raises a thorny general question. How is it that in
their most concrete, ground-floor employment, concepts like *will
be, was, correct, must, make, prevent* and *fault* behave, in the main,

with exemplary docility, but become wild when employed in what are mere first-floor generalizations of their ground-floor employments? We are in very little danger of giving or taking the wrong logical change in our daily marketing uses of 'tomorrow' and 'yesterday'. We know perfectly well how to make our daily sales and purchases with them. Yet in the general case, when we try to negotiate with 'what is', 'what is to be', 'what was' and 'what was to be' we very easily get our accounts in a muddle. We are quite at home with 'therefore' and all at sea with 'necessary'. How is it that we get our accounts in a muddle when we try to do wholesale business with ideas with which in retail trade we operate quite efficiently every day of our lives? Later on I hope to give something of an answer to this question. For the moment I merely advertise it.

Meanwhile there is another feature of the issue to which we should attend. I have indicated that the quandary, though relatively simple, does depend upon a smallish number of concepts, namely, in the first instance, upon those of *event, before* and *after, truth, necessity, cause, prevention, fault* and *responsibility*. Now there is not just one of these concepts which is the logical trouble-maker. The trouble arises out of the interplay between all of them. The litigation between the two initial platitudes involves a whole web of conflicting interests. There is not just a single recalcitrant knot in the middle of one of the concepts involved. All the strings between all of them are implicated in the one tangle.

I mention this point because some people have got the idea from some of the professions though not, I think, the practices of philosophers, that doing philosophy consists or should consist of untying logical knots one at a time—as if, to burlesque the idea, it would have been quite proper and feasible for Hume on Monday to analyse the use of the term 'cause', and then on Tuesday, Wednesday and Thursday to move on to analyse *seriatim* the uses of the terms 'causeway', 'cautery' and 'caution', in alphabetical order.

I have no special objection to or any special liking for the fashion of describing as 'analysis' the sort or sorts of conceptual examination which constitute philosophizing. But the idea is totally false that this examination is a sort of garage inspection of one conceptual vehicle at a time. On the contrary, to put it dogmatically, it is always a traffic-inspector's examination of a conceptual traffic-block, involving at least two streams of vehicles hailing from the theories, or points of view or platitudes which are at cross-purposes with one another.

One other point arises in connexion with this last one. The child can be taught a lot of words, one after another; or, when consulting the dictionary to find out the meanings of some unfamiliar words in a difficult passage, he can look up these words separately in alphabetical or any other order. This fact, among others, has encouraged the notion that the ideas or concepts conveyed by these words are something like separately movable and examinable chessmen, coins, counters, snapshots—or words. But we should not think of what a word conveys as if it were, like the word, a sort of counter, though unlike the word, an invisible counter. Consider a wicket-keeper. He is an individual, who can be fetched out of the team and separately interviewed, photographed or massaged. But his role in the game, namely the wicket-keeping that he does, so interlocks with what the other cricketers do, that if they stopped playing, he could not go on keeping wicket. He alone performs his particular role, yet he cannot perform it alone. For him to keep wicket, there must be a wicket, a pitch, a ball, a bat, a bowler and a batsman. Even that is not enough. There must be a game in progress and not, for example, a funeral, a fight or a dance; and the game must be a game of cricket and not, for example, a game of 'Touch Last'. The same man who keeps wicket on Saturday may play tennis on Sunday. But he cannot keep wicket in a game of tennis. He can switch from one set of sporting functions to another, but one of his functions cannot be switched to the other game. In much the same way, concepts are not things, as words are, but rather the functionings of words, as keeping wicket is the functioning of the wicket-keeper. Very much as the functioning of the wicket-keeper interlocks with the functioning of the bowler, the batsman and the rest, so the functioning of a word interlocks with the functioning of the other members of the team for which that word is playing. One word may have two or more functions; but one of its functions cannot change places with another.

Let me illustrate. A game like Bridge or Poker has a fairly elaborate and well-organized technical vocabulary, as in different degrees have nearly all games, crafts, professions, hobbies and sciences. Naturally the technical terms peculiar to Bridge have to be learned. How do we learn them? One thing is clear. We do not and could not master the use of one of them without yet having begun to learn the use of any of the others. It would be absurd to try to teach a boy how to use the concept of *cross-ruff*, without yet having introduced him to the notions of *following suit, trump* and *partner*. But if he has been introduced to the way these terms function together in Bridge talk, then he has begun to learn some of the elements of Bridge. Or consider the technical dictions of English lawyers. Could a student claim to understand one or seven of its specialist terms, though knowing nothing of the law? or claim to know the law while not understanding at least a considerable fraction of its terminological apparatus? The terminological apparatus of a science is in the same way a team and not a mere mob of terms. The part played by one of them belongs, with the parts played by the others, to the particular game or work of the whole apparatus. A person who had merely memorized the dictionary-paraphrases of a thousand technical terms of physics or economics would not yet have begun to be a physicist or an economist. He would not yet have learned how to operate with those terms. So he would not yet understand them. If he cannot yet think any of the thoughts of economic theory, he has not yet got any of its special concepts.

What is true of the more or less highly technical terms of games, the law, the sciences, the trades and professions is true also, with important modifications, of the terms of everyday discourse. These stand to the terms of the specialists very much as civilians stand to the officers, non-commissioned officers and private soldiers of different units in the Army. The rights, duties and privileges of soldiers are carefully prescribed; their uniforms, badges, stripes and buttons show their ranks, trades and units; drill, discipline and daily orders mould their movements. But civilians too have their codes, their habits, and their etiquettes; their work, pay and taxes tend to be regular; their social circles, their apparel and their amusements, though not regimented, are pretty stable. We know, too, how in this twentieth century of ours the distinctions between civilians and soldiers are notoriously blurred. Similarly the line between un-technical and technical dictions is a blurred line, and one frequently crossed in both directions; and though untechnical terms have not got their functions officially imposed upon them, they have their functions, privileges and immunities none the less. They resemble civilians rather than soldiers, but most of them also resemble rate-payers rather than gipsies.

The functions of technical terms, that is, the concepts conveyed by them, are more or less severely regimented. The kinds of interplay of function for which they are built are relatively definite and circumscribed. Yet untechnical terms, too, though they belong to no single organized unit, still have their individual places in indefinitely many overlapping and intermingling *milieus*.

It can be appreciated, consequently, that the functions of terms become both narrower and better prescribed as they become more official. Their roles in discourse can be more strictly formulated as their commitments are reduced in number and in scope. Hence, the more exactly their duties come to being fixed by charters and commissions, the further they move from being philosophically interesting. The official concepts of Bridge generate few if any logical puzzles. Disputes could not be settled or rubbers won if they were generated. Logical puzzles arise especially over concepts that are uncommissioned, namely the civilian concepts which, instead of having been conscripted and trained for just one definite and appointed niche in one organized unit, have grown up into their special but unappointed places in a thousand unchartered groups and informal associations. This is why an issue like the fatalist issue, though starting with a quite slender stem, ramifies out so swiftly into seemingly remote sectors of human interests. The question whether statements in the future tense can be true swiftly opened out into, among a thousand others, the question whether anything is gained by learning to swim.

Certain thinkers, properly impressed by the excellent logical discipline of the technical concepts of long-established and well consolidated sciences like pure mathematics and mechanics, have urged that intellectual progress is impeded by the survival of the unofficial concepts of unspecialized thought; as if there were something damagingly amateurish or infantile in the businesses and avocations of unconscripted civilians. Members of the Portland Club, the M.C.C., or the Law Faculty of a University might, with even greater justice, contrast their own scrupulously pruned and even carpentered terms of art with the undesigned dictions of everyday discourse. It is, of course, quite true that scientific, legal or financial thinking could not be conducted only in colloquial idioms. But it is quite false that people could, even in Utopia, be given their first lessons in talking and thinking in the terms of this or that technical apparatus. Fingers and feet are, for many special purposes, grossly inefficient instruments. But to replace the infant's fingers and feet by pliers and pedals would not be a good plan—especially as the employment of pliers and pedals themselves depends upon the employment of fingers and feet. Nor does the specialist when he comes to use the designed terms of his art cease to depend upon the concepts which he began to master in the nursery, any more than the driver, whose skill and interests are concentrated on the mechanically complex and delicate works of his car, cease to avail himself of the mechanically crude properties of the public highway. He could not use his car without using the roads, though he could, as the pedestrian that he often is, use these same roads without using his car.

III

ACHILLES AND THE TORTOISE

I sʜᴀʟʟ now discuss a dilemma which I imagine is familiar to everybody. It is quite certain that a fast runner following a slow runner will overtake him in the end. We can calculate by simple arithmetic after what distance and after what time the chase will be over, given only the initial distance and the speeds of the two runners. The chase will be over in the time it would take to cover the initial interval at the speed of the fast runner minus the speed of the slow runner. The distance covered by the pursuer by the end of the chase is calculable from his actual speed over the ground and the time for which he runs. Nothing could be more decisively settled. Yet there is a very different answer which also seems to follow with equal cogency from the same data. Achilles is in pursuit of the tortoise and before he catches him he has to reach the tortoise's starting-line, by which time the tortoise has advanced a little way ahead of this line. So Achilles has now to make up this new, reduced lead and does so; but by the time he has done this, the tortoise has once again got a little bit further ahead. Ahead of each lead that Achilles makes up, there always remains a further, though always diminished lead for him still to make up. There is no number of such leads at the end of which no lead remains to be made up. So Achilles never catches the tortoise. He whittles down the distance, but never whittles it down to nothing. Notice that at each stage the tortoise's lead is a finite one. If Achilles has whittled off ten or a thousand such ever dwindling leads one after another, the lead still to be made up is of finite length. We cannot say that after such and such a number of stages, the tortoise's lead will have shrunk to the dimensions of an Euclidean point. If Achilles takes any time at all to make up a lead, he gives time for the tortoise to get some way past the terminus of that lead. The same result follows if we consider intervals of time instead of distances in space. At the end of the period taken to make up one lead, there remains another diminished period in which Achilles has to make up the next lead. There is no finite number of such ever-diminishing overtaking-periods, such that we can say that after 100 or 1000 of them, no further period of pursuing remains.

This is one of the justly famous paradoxes of Zeno. In many ways it deserves to rank as the paradigm of a philosophical puzzle. It clearly is a philosophical puzzle and not an arithmetical problem. No solution is to be looked for by going over, with greater care, the calculations by which it is established that Achilles will catch the tortoise in, say, exactly six minutes. But nor is a solution to be found by reconsidering the argument proving that lead 1 plus lead 2, plus lead 3, etc., never add up to the total distance to be covered by Achilles in order to catch the tortoise. There is no number, such as a million, such that after a million of these dwindling leads have been made up, no lead remains to be made up.

I shall try to expose just where Zeno's argument seems to prove one thing, namely that the chase cannot end, but really proves, perfectly validly, a different and undisturbing conclusion; and also to show why the difference between this real and that apparent conclusion is in an interesting way a queerly elusive one. It is the elusiveness of this difference which makes it so excellent a specimen of a logical dilemma.

In offering a solution of this paradox, I expect to meet the fate of so many who have tried before, namely demonstrable failure. But for my general purpose this will not matter. I shall have exhibited that the argument is a tricky one, and brought out for consideration some of the factors which make it tricky. Even if I fail, I may with luck have betrayed, without knowing it, some factor which has succeeded in tricking me.

First, let us notice some seemingly trivial points which the two conflicting treatments of the race have in common, or seem to have in common. To make the question definite, let us suppose that Achilles runs at eleven miles an hour, while the tortoise crawls at one mile an hour, and that the tortoise has a start of one mile. According to the natural treatment, the race will be over in the time that it would have taken Achilles to reach the tortoise if the tortoise had not budged at all, and Achilles had run at ten miles an hour instead of eleven miles an hour; i.e. the race will be over in one-tenth of an hour, or six minutes. As Achilles runs for six minutes at eleven miles an hour, the

distance he will have covered is eleven tenths of a mile, i.e. a mile
and a tenth of a mile. This calculation is done in terms of miles
and fractions of miles, and in hours and fractions of hours, namely
minutes. But obviously it would have made no difference had we
instead worked the distances out in yards and inches, or metres
and centimetres, or if we had worked out the times in seconds or
in fractions of a year.

The same thing is true of Zeno's treatment of the race. The
racers start a mile apart (or 1760 yards apart or 5280 feet or the
corresponding number of metres or centimetres). While Achilles
runs the initial mile, the tortoise crawls his fraction of a mile,
namely one eleventh of a·mile; while Achilles is covering this
next fraction of a mile, the tortoise is crawling his next fraction
of that fraction of a mile, and so on. For each successive lead
that Achilles has made up, the tortoise has established a new lead
of his regular fraction of the length of the one before.

That is to say, in both treatments our calculations are calculations of distances and parts of those distances, e.g. miles and
elevenths of a mile, or furlongs and elevenths of a furlong; or
they are calculations of stretches of time and parts of those
stretches, e.g. hours and fractions of hours or minutes and
fractions of minutes.

According to the natural treatment, the race is over in six
minutes. Its duration consisted of the first minute, plus the
second minute, plus the third... up to six. These parts of that
duration duly add up to the whole. If instead we partition the
duration of the race into seconds, it would come to 360 seconds,
and these 360 parts duly add up to the whole six minutes.
Similarly the total distance run by Achilles is a mile and a tenth
or, if you prefer, 1936 yards; and the tenths of a mile covered
(or the yards) duly add up to the total.

Here I am simply reminding you of the platitude that a whole
is the sum of its parts, or that $\frac{12}{12} = 1$, or $\frac{1936}{1936} = 1$, or, generally,
whatever number x stands for, $\frac{x}{x} = 1$.

But to our consternation according to Zeno's treatment of
the race, this platitude seems to break down. Here again we
have stretches of space and sub-stretches of it, or stretches of

time and sub-stretches of it. Yet here the slices that we have cut off refuse to add up to the whole distance or the whole duration. The first lead that Achilles makes up, plus the second, plus the third... never add up to the distance required for him to have caught the tortoise. Wholes surely are sums of their parts, yet here are parts of a whole which, however numerous, never amount to that whole. Or a whole *is* all of its parts taken together; yet here we have as many parts as we like, but such that we can at no stage say that we have now taken together all of them. For there is at every stage a part left outstanding.

Let us consider, for a moment, the slices into which a cake may be cut. Cut the cake into six or sixty slices, and these six or sixty slices, taken together, constitute the entire cake. The cake is its six sixths or its sixty sixtieths. But now suppose that the mother of a family chooses instead to circulate an uncut cake round the table, instructing the children that each is to cut off a bit and only a bit of what is on the cake-plate; i.e. that no child is to take the whole of what he finds on the plate. Then, obviously, so long as her instructions are observed, however far and often the cake circulates, there is always a bit of cake left. If they obey her orders always to leave a bit, then they always leave a bit. Or to put it the other way round, if they obey her orders never to take the whole of the last fragment, a fragment always remains untaken. What they have taken off the cake-plate never constitutes the whole cake. Certainly what they take at each helping is a part—a steadily diminishing part—of the whole cake. But the cake is, at any selected stage, not merely the sum of these consumed parts. None the less it really is the sum of these consumed parts *plus the unconsumed part*. This addition sum works out correctly at each stage at which the cake-plate is passed on. At that moment the pieces already taken plus the fragment still untaken do constitute the whole cake. Similarly at the next stage, and the next. But at no stage is the unconsumed residue not a proper part of the cake; so at no stage do the parts consumed amount to all of the parts of the cake. This is simply the platitude that a whole is more than the sum of *all of its parts but one*, however small that one may be. The mother's second method of cake-partition ensured that there should be at every stage such a part left on the cake-plate, though one of smaller and smaller dimensions with each stage of the division.

She could make her instructions more precise. She now passes the plate round the children in order of decreasing seniority, and in order that bigger children shall have the bigger portions, she instructs the children always to take not just a bit but exactly half and so to leave just half of what is on the plate. The first child begins with a half cake, and leaves a half, the second gets a quarter, and leaves a quarter, the third gets an eighth, and leaves an eighth, and so on. The plate never stops circulating. After each cut there remains a morsel to be bisected by the next child. Obviously the children's patience or their eyesight will give out before the cake gives out. For the cake cannot give out on this principle of division.

Notice again, that while the slices taken at no stage amount to the whole cake, yet at each stage the slices so far taken *plus the morsel still untaken* certainly do amount to the whole cake. These slices taken plus the morsel remaining can be counted, so that at each stage we can speak in the ordinary way of all the parts of the cake, namely, say, all the 99 slices already taken plus the one morsel now outstanding, i.e. 100 bits in all. At the next stage the scope of the 'all' will be different. It will now be all the 100 slices taken plus the crumb now outstanding, i.e. 101 bits in all. There is another point to be borne in mind for future use. The size of each slice, if the bisection is exact, is a measurable and cal-culable fraction of the size of the original whole cake; the first slice to be eaten was a half-cake, the second was a quarter-cake, the third was an eighth of the cake, and so on. The sizes of the slices are fixed in terms of the size of the cake. The partition-method employed was from the start a method of operating upon the cake as a whole. So if, say, the second child, playing the Zeno, were to say 'What we consume never amounts to the whole cake; so I believe that there never was a whole cake of finite size to consume', he could be refuted by being asked what his own first slice was one-quarter of. There must have been the whole cake, for him to get a quarter of it; and a finite one, for his quarter of it was finite. Or he could be asked what it is, according to him, that the parts consumed never amount to.

I now want to satisfy you that the race between Achilles and the tortoise exemplifies just what is exemplified by the mother's division of the cake by the second method.

In order both to simplify the story and to bring it into parallel with the second method of dividing the cake, let us now say that Achilles saunters at two miles an hour, the tortoise crawls at one mile an hour, and has a start of one mile. Since the difference between their speeds is one mile an hour, Achilles will catch the tortoise in one hour, by which time he will have covered two miles of the race-track. Now we spectators of the race might, after the event, go back over this two-mile course of his and plant a flag in the ground at the end of each of the eight quarter-miles, or each of the sixteen furlongs that Achilles had run. Our last flag would then be planted where the race ended. But now suppose that, when the race is over, we go back over these two miles of the track covered by Achilles, and choose instead to stick one flag into the ground where Achilles started, a second at the half-way point of his total course, a third at the half-way point of the second half of his course, a fourth at the half-way point of the outstanding quarter of his course, and so on. Clearly for every flag we plant, there is always another flag to put in half-way between it and the place where Achilles caught the tortoise. (In fact, of course, we shall soon reach a point where our flags are too bulky for us to continue the operation.) We shall never be able to plant a flag just at the place where the race ended, since our principle of flag-planting was that each flag was to be planted half-way between the last flag planted and the place where the race ended. In effect our instructions were to plant each flag ahead of the last one but also behind the terminus of the race. If we obey these instructions, it follows that we never plant a flag which is not behind the terminus, and so that we never plant the last flag. At no stage does the distance between Achilles' start-line and the last flag to be planted amount to the whole distance run by Achilles. But conversely, at each stage the total distance run by Achilles does consist of the sum of all the distances between the flags *plus the distance between the last flag planted and the point where the race ended.* Achilles' whole course is not the sum of all of its parts but one; it is the sum of all of those flagged parts plus the outstanding unflagged one. The number of these stretches alters and the length of both the last stretch to be flagged and the remainder-stretch alters with each new flag that is planted. At one stage, $\frac{15}{16}$ of his course has been flagged and $\frac{1}{16}$ of his course is still ahead of the last flag planted, and $\frac{15}{16} + \frac{1}{16}$ duly $= 1$. At the next stage $\frac{31}{32}$ of his course has been flagged and $\frac{1}{32}$ of his course is still ahead of the last flag planted; but again $\frac{31}{32} + \frac{1}{32}$ duly $= 1$.

No great mystery seems to confront us here. If we obey the instruction always to leave room for one more flag, we always leave room for one more flag. Nor can the fact that no flag is the last flag persuade us that Achilles' course was endless, since we knowingly began our flag-planting operations with the datum that his was a two-mile course, the start-line and the terminus of which we knew. The places where we planted our flags were fixed in terms of just this two-mile course, namely one flag at its midpoint, the next at the end of its third half-mile, the next at the end of its fourteenth furlong and so on. We were, all the time, planting flags to mark out determinate portions of the precise two-mile course that Achilles ran. We could, if we had chosen, have worked backwards on the same principle from the terminus of the race; and then we should never get a flag planted on his start-line. Yet this would not persuade us that a race had a finish, but no beginning.

What the distances flagged fail at each stage to amount to is the two-mile distance that he had run by the time he caught the tortoise, just because this distance is, according to the instructions, the sum of those flagged distances plus whatever un-flagged distance remains outstanding.

It is easy now to see that the flags planted according to these instructions do in fact mark precisely the termini of those successive leads established by the tortoise on which Zeno made us concentrate. From Achilles' start-line to the tortoise's start-line was just the mile between the first flag that we planted and the second. Where the tortoise was, when Achilles reached this half-way point of his total course, is the place where we planted our flag for the third quarter of Achilles' total chase, and so on. What we measure off after the event with a surveyor's chain and, later on, a micrometer, Achilles might in principle, though not in practice, have measured off by running steadily at twice the tortoise's speed and by marking, in his mind, the termini of the tortoise's successive leads. If informed that he was going at twice the tortoise's speed, then Achilles himself could have known, while running, that the terminus of the first lead was the midpoint of his pursuit, that the terminus of the tortoise's second lead marked the third quarter of his pursuit, that the next marked the seventh eighth of his pursuit, and so on. Given their actual speeds, he would have known that he would catch the tortoise at the second milestone, and so that the successive leads were determinate portions of what was going to be his two-mile chase. But we are induced to imagine that Achilles was without these data by the fact that in ordinary races the runners do not know just how fast they or their opponents are running; they do not know that their opponents are not accelerating or decelerating or just about to stop or even to start coming backwards. But had he known what we are allowed to know, that his and his opponent's speeds were constant, and that his speed was twice his opponent's, then he himself could have used his own progress from lead-terminus to lead-terminus as, so to speak, a moving surveyor's chain; and he could have recognized the termini of the successive leads that he had to make up as doing just what our flags do, namely as marking off determinate slices of his total course from start-line to the terminus of his pursuit. The series of these diminishing leads would then have felt to him not like an endless sequence of postponements of victory but like, what of course they were, measured stages towards his calculable victory. Just this is part of Zeno's trick. Zeno professed to be trying to build up Achilles' total course out of this series of leads made up, where we have been dividing up Achilles' total two-mile course, taken as our datum, by a flag-planting procedure each stage of which was, by rule, non-ultimate. We chose to apply a special partition-procedure to a known and determinate stretch of a race-track, namely the two miles of it that Achilles ran; we cannot, therefore, be browbeaten by the interminableness of the task of flag-planting into doubting whether Achilles' pursuit had a terminus. Zeno, ingeniously, started at the other end. By talking in terms of distances still to be covered by Achilles, he got the endlessness of this series of leads to browbeat Achilles and us into doubting whether he could catch the tortoise at all. Yet the termini of the

successive leads that Achilles has to make up according to Zeno's
account come exactly where we planted our flags to mark out
our regularly diminishing but determinate slices of Achilles
precise two-mile course to victory. In other words, Zeno has,
ingeniously, got us to look at our flag-system back to front,
rather as if the mother told her children that she had made her
cake that morning by assembling the eldest child's half-cake, the
second child's quarter-cake, the third child's eighth, and so on—
a story which they would quickly see through, not only because
the morsel still on the cake-plate is going to be left out of her
inventory, but also because in her very mention of the eldest
child's half-cake and the second child's quarter-cake, and so on,
she had already been referring to the whole cake, as that whole
of which their determinate portions had been those determinate
portions. Similarly Zeno, in his mentions of the successive leads
to be made up by Achilles, is, though surreptitiously and only by
implication, referring to the total two-mile course run by
Achilles in overtaking the tortoise; or in other words, his
argument itself rests on the unadvertised premiss that Achilles
does catch the tortoise in, say, precisely two miles and in precisely one hour. For he has told us that Achilles is overtaking
the tortoise at one mile an hour, and that the initial lead was one
mile. As I said, the reason why at first sight this does not seem
to be the case is that we are induced to look at the race through
Achilles' own eyes. He can see, we suppose, where the tortoise's
start-line is all the way from his own start-line. As he reaches
the tortoise's start-line, he can see the terminus of the new lead
that the tortoise has now established, and so on. But he cannot
at any stage see a tape to be broken by the winner of the race,
since what in this race corresponds to reaching the tape in
an ordinary side-by-side race, is his catching up with the tortoise,
and where on the race-track this will occur is not a visible
feature of the track. So, unless he knows what we have been told,
he cannot be thinking of the successive leads as calculable
fractions of his eventual total course, in the way in which the
mother, if she has kept count, can calculate the weights of the
successive portions cut off the cake as specified fractions of the
weight of the original cake. She weighed the cake before tea;
Achilles did not measure his run before he made it, and we are

induced to assume that he could not know its length while running it. The mother, knowing the weight of the cake and the scrupulousness of the bisection of the slices taken, can, just by keeping count of the cuts, also keep tally, stage by stage, of the weights of the slices removed and thence of the weight of the remainder of the cake on the cake-plate. But Achilles who does not, we naturally assume, know precisely his own speed or that of the tortoise, even if he does know the exact length of the tortoise's start, cannot work out exactly when he has covered the first half, the first three-quarters, the first seven-eighths, etc., of what will have been his total course to victory. If we gave him our flags to drop as he reached these points, he would not know just where to drop them. Yet if he does drop them just at the terminus of each of the leads which Zeno describes him as making up, one after the other, he will in fact unwittingly have dropped them just where we, after the event, would have deliberately planted them. Our chosen principle of flag-planting is just the obverse of the facts, which presumably Achilles does not know, that his speed is double that of the tortoise, and so that the tortoise's one-mile start constitutes just half of what is to be Achilles' total course. The lengths of the successive leads that Achilles has to make up are necessarily proportional to the difference between the speeds of the two competitors. Achilles himself is more nearly in the position of the mother, if she had instructed her children merely to take a bit and leave a bit of whatever remains on the plate, without prescribing any scale for these bits. She cannot now calculate the actual weight of the portions consumed or of the portion still unconsumed. But she still knows that at each stage the combined weights of the consumed portions and the unconsumed portion, whatever these may be, add up to the weight of the original cake.

Similarly the whole of the course that Achilles will have run is indeed the sum of as many parts as we or he may care to slice off it plus the part that we or he have left on it. The fact that these parts are of diminishing length, on this principle of partition, is of no more interest than the fact that the parts were all of the same length on our first principle of partition. As a cake is not five of the six slices into which it has been cut, but those five plus the remaining sixth slice, so Achilles' course is not the sum of the half, plus the quarter, plus the eighth of it, etc., that we have at this or that stage chosen to put on one side, but it is the sum of these plus the remainder. Nor is this remainder one of mysterious or elusive dimensions. It is of exactly the same dimensions as the last fraction that we sliced off before we chose to stop slicing.

Certainly, if we choose to conduct our slicing according to the principle that a remainder shall always be left, a remainder is always left. That this division can go on *ad infinitum* is an alarming phrase, but it means no more than that after each cut, a remainder is left to divide by a subsequent cut. But the consoling truth remains that whether we stop after two cuts or after two hundred, the whole off which we were cutting is the sum of what we have cut off it, plus what we have left.

To put a central point very crudely, we have to distinguish the question 'How many portions have you cut *off* the object?' from the question 'How many portions have you cut it *into*?' The answer to the second question is higher by one than the answer to the first. The platitude 'a whole is the sum of its parts' means that a whole is the sum of the portions you cut it into; it does not mean, what is false, that it is the sum of the portions you have cut off it, if this phrase implies that something remains. Zeno gets us and Achilles to think of each of the successive leads that are to be made up as portions which ought somehow to add up, but cannot add up, to the total course he has to run. He thus averts our attention from the fact that these successive leads were, in effect, selected by Achilles for being only slices cut off the distance he has yet to run, i.e. for making up that total distance *minus* something. His principle of selection presupposes that there is the total distance which he has got to run—else there would be nothing for him to select as an intermediate slice of that distance. Suppose that as Achilles reaches the first milestone he sees the tortoise at the next half-mile post. According to Zeno, he argues despondently 'I have got to reach that half-mile post first and still run on a bit further in order to catch the tortoise'. But his argument assumes that he knows that the tortoise is not going to stop crawling at the half-mile post. If he does stop there, he will be caught there. Achilles is then supposed not only to know that the tortoise is now at that half-mile post but also to assume that he is going past it, i.e. to assume that the half-mile post marks only some fraction of the distance to the terminus of the race. That there is a definite distance to that terminus is presupposed by his assumption that the half-mile post is only a part of that distance, i.e. that a lead to be made up is a stage towards the finish of the race, and therefore not the whole of the distance to that point.

Of course, if it is an ordinary race, Achilles may not catch the tortoise at all. He will not do so if he himself so slows down or the tortoise so accelerates that there is now no difference between their speeds, or else a difference in the tortoise's favour. But this is only to say that Achilles cannot overtake the tortoise without going faster than the tortoise—a thing which we and he never doubted. If the race does take this unfavourable turn, then the next half-mile post will indeed not mark a part of Achilles' total course to victory, since there is going to be no victory. It does mark off a part of his total course to victory, if and only if Achilles is in fact overtaking and going on overtaking the tortoise—a condition which was granted to us by Zeno, though perhaps not imparted to Achilles. So we assume that Achilles cannot know that the next lead to be made up is a definite fraction of what will be his total course to victory, since he does not know that he will win or that his speed is to be constant at twice that of the tortoise. But we have, by implication, been told that he will win, so we know that this lead, and the next and the next, are definite fractions of his total course to victory. But we were induced to put this knowledge into cold storage by being led to look at the race through Achilles' eyes. We were trying to envisage our surveyor's task through the haze of a runner's doubts, ignorances and despondencies. So we thought of his course as composed of an échelon of diminishing, intermediate stages, each of which, because intermediate, was therefore non-ultimate. We forgot, what we knew all the time, what these stages were intermediate between, namely between Achilles' start-line and the place where he caught the tortoise. We forgot that what is cut off the cake is not what the cake is cut into, and that as what had at each stage been cut off it was measured or calculable, so what, at that stage, the cake had been cut into was measurable or calculable.

Now let us draw some general lessons from this dilemma.

First of all, though it is presented in the dramatic form of a foot-race under Greek skies between two rather engaging characters, its argument is of quite general application. A race involves the covering of a distance in a time. Part of our confusion was due to our wondering whether we ought to be concentrating on furlongs or on minutes. But the argument applies where there is no question of the passage of time, as, for example, in the case of the progressive bisection of a cake. It applies, too, where there is no question of stretches of space, as, for example, in the case of an initially cool thermometer overtaking the rising temperature of the contents of a saucepan, or a clever junior overtaking the scholarship-level of a senior boy whose scholarship is improving too, though less rapidly.

Next, in this particular issue we are trying to find out after what stretch of time and after what distance Achilles overtakes the tortoise, or else, if scared by Zeno, we are trying to find out if there is any stretch of time or any distance at the end of which Achilles has overtaken him. In both cases we are thinking about or intellectually operating upon slices of a day and slices of a chase. In other applications we might be thinking about (or operating upon) slices of cake, or degrees of temperature.

But in an important way we are, in all applications, thinking *in terms of* or operating *with* the same overarching notions of *part*, *whole*, *fraction*, *total*, *plus*, *minus* and *multiplied by*. It is because we have already learned to execute some abstract manœuvres with these notions, i.e. sums in simple arithmetic, that we are capable of calculating when a man will catch a tortoise and capable, too, of being embarrassed by an argument which seems to prove that he will never do so. A boy who has run and witnessed many races, but cannot yet grasp the abstract platitude that a whole is the sum of its parts, cannot yet work out how many quarter-miles there are in a two-mile course, nor can he grasp the other abstract platitude that the portions cut off something at no stage amount to the whole of that thing.

But now consider the boy who has reached the stage of dealing clear-headedly in simple, abstract arithmetic, not only with fractions, and their addition and subtraction, but also with the multiplication of fractions. He realizes well enough, in the abstract, that not merely does $\frac{2}{3} \times \frac{2}{3}$ come to something less than 1, but even fractions like $\frac{9}{10} \times \frac{9}{10}$ or $\frac{999}{1000} \times \frac{999}{1000}$ come to something less than 1, and less even than either of the fractions themselves. Yet when the family cake is cut, not according to the usual principle of dividing it into six or ten more or less equal slices, but according to the unusual principle of so dividing it, that each cut divides the remainder in a given ratio, he may still get the feeling that the cake has been transformed into a magic cake, a cake which allows itself to be cut at and cut at for ever. It now seems to be an inexhaustible cake, and yet inexhaustible in a disappointing way, since the family gets no more cake, indeed somewhat less cake, than it did when it was cut in the usual way. Though there is always more cake to come, yet the cake has visibly not, like the Hydra, repaired its losses. That is to say, though he knows how to apply to such things as cakes, or two-mile stretches of a race-track, the simple, abstract notions of fractions and sums of fractions, he is not yet clear about the application to cakes or race-tracks of the more complex abstract notion of the products of fractions. He cannot clearly distinguish between the inexhaustibleness of a magic cake or a magic race-track which repairs its losses, and the inexhaustibleness of the series of a fraction of an ordinary cake or race-track plus that fraction of the remainder, plus that fraction of the remainder.... Confusedly, he attributes to the cake or race-track a difference from ordinary cakes and race-tracks, which is really a difference between one division procedure and another division procedure. He ascribes a queer endlessness to Achilles' pursuit of the tortoise, where he should have ascribed an uninteresting non-finality to each of the stages of a certain, special way of subdividing two miles.

He is behaving somewhat like the boy who, having learned one card game, namely 'Snap', when he comes to a new cardgame, like Whist, cannot for a while help assimilating what he has to do with his cards now to the things he has long since learned to do with those same cards in 'Snap'. He is put out at finding that play which works in 'Snap', does not work in Whist, and vice versa. Yet, in a way, he *has* learned the rules of

Whist—he has learned them well enough for some purposes, but
not well enough to be safe from relapsing now and again into
'Snap' play and 'Snap' thinking. After all, the cards he is
playing with now are the same old cards.

This point brings us back to a suggestion that I made in the
previous chapter, but left for later expansion. The collision
between the natural view that Achilles catches the tortoise after
a pursuit of measurable and calculable length and the queer view
that he never catches him at all, does not occur while we are
thinking at ground-floor level of such things as Achilles' paces,
the dusty furlongs of the track and the tortoise's inferior speed.
It occurs when we reach the first-floor level of thinking, on
which we try to work out if and when Achilles will catch the
tortoise by procedures of calculation which are of quite general
application. The pony is docile enough in its home paddock. It is
when we try to drive him in some standardized conceptual
harness that his habits and our intentions conflict, even though
we have got quite used to the pony's behaviour in the paddock
and, also, but separately, quite used in the harness-room to the
construction and assemblage of the harness. Handling this
conceptual pony in this conceptual harness involves us in
troubles, for which we cannot fix the blame on either the pony
or the harness. These excellent reins get under that excellent
pony's hooves. How is what we know quite well about the stages
of an athlete's victorious pursuit to be married with what we also
know quite well about the results of adding together a fraction
of a whole, that fraction of the remainder, that fraction of the
next remainder, and so on?

For example, Zeno's argument seems to prove that Achilles
never catches the tortoise—never, in the sense that years,
centuries, millennia after the start of the race Achilles will still
be in hopeless pursuit; that the race is an eternal race, like the
pursuit by a donkey of the carrot suspended in front of his nose.
But this sense of 'never', in which all eternity is occupied in vain
pursuit, is quite different from the sense of 'never', in which we
say, when talking arithmetic, that the sum of $\frac{1}{2}$, $\frac{1}{4}$, $\frac{1}{8}$, $\frac{1}{16}$, etc.,
never amounts to unity. To say this is simply to utter the general
proposition that any particular remainder-bisection leaves a
remainder to bisect. The only connexion that this 'never' has

with the 'never' of all eternity is that if a silly computer were to attempt to continue bisecting remainders until he had found one which was halved but had no second half, his attempt would then go on to all eternity. Such a computer would indeed resemble the donkey pursuing a carrot which is suspended in front of his nose. But the arithmetical proposition itself says nothing about silly or sensible computers. It itself is not disheartening prophecy, for it is not a prophecy at all; it is just a general truth about a fraction.

A similar ambiguity belongs to the word 'all'. When a cake is divided in the ordinary way into six or sixty portions, we can speak of all these portions, and enumerate them. There are six or sixty of them in all. We have a countable total and it amounts to the whole cake. When the cake is divided according to the less usual principle, that each bit taken shall be only a fraction of what remained after the previous cut, then again we can use the word 'all' or 'total' in this same manner. We can talk about and enumerate the bits already taken at stage 3, or the bits already taken at stage 7 and so on. Here the bits already removed at this or that specified stage do not amount to the whole cake. At this or that given stage, what amount to the whole cake is the, still countable, total of the bits removed plus the one bit still on the plate. But for certain purposes we want to stand back from this or that specified stage of the division-process, and to talk about the procession of these stages. For example we want to say, quite generally, that all the cuts leave residues to be cut. Now here the 'all' is not a countable total—and it is not an uncountable total either. For it is not a total. What it expresses can be expressed just as well by 'any', namely 'any cut leaves a residue to be cut'.

That is, in the first use of 'all' we could, in principle, fill out with 'all six...', or 'all sixty...'. In this second use of 'all' we could not fill out with 'all (so and so many)...'. Not because there are *too* many, but because 'any...' carries, *ex officio*, the notion of 'no matter which...', and this is not a totality-notion of any sort, familiar or queer.

Unfortunately for us, we have here had to use both notions together, both that of 'all (so and so many)...' and that of 'any (no matter which)...'. For we have to say that at any

stage (no matter which), all the x bits then removed amount to
something less than the whole cake; or that at any stage, no
matter which, the total of the x bits taken plus the one bit
untaken does amount to the whole cake.

We talk about a race in one tone of voice, we talk arithmetic
in another tone of voice; but in talking the arithmetic of a race
we have to mix our tones of voice, and in doing this we may
easily feel—and even speak as if—we were talking out of different sides of our mouths at the same time.

We decide factual questions about the length and duration of
a race by one procedure, namely measurement; we decide
arithmetical questions by another procedure, namely calculation.
But then, given some facts about the race established by
measurement, we can decide other questions about that race by
calculations applied to these measurements. The two procedures
of settling the different sorts of questions intertwine, somehow,
into a procedure for establishing by calculation concrete,
measurable facts about this particular race. We have the pony in
the harness that was meant for any such pony, yet we can mis-
manage the previously quite manageable pony in its previously
quite manageable harness. Two separate skills do not, in the
beginning, intertwine into one conjoint skill.

Looking back, now, at the fatalist imbroglio which we
expressed in the slogan 'Whatever is, always was to be', we
can see without difficulty that here too our trouble was a sort of
pony-harness trouble. The platitude that whatever happens
would have fulfilled any prior guess to the effect that it would
happen was a logician's platitude. It gave us no news about
what happens, but it told us a truism about what it is for a statement in the future tense to come true. On the other hand, the
platitudes that many things that happen are our fault and that
there are some catastrophes which can and others which cannot
be averted, these are not logicians' truisms, but truisms about
the world and human beings. Very crudely, they are nursemaids'
truisms. In attempting to harness the nursemaid's to the
logician's truisms, we lost control and found ourselves ascribing
to actions and happenings properties which can belong only to
the stock in trade of logicians, namely statements or propositions. We were talking in the logician's tone of voice about

what makes things happen, and then in the nursemaid's tone of voice about connexions between truths. Similarly here we have been talking, so to speak, in one breath with the sporting reporter of a newspaper, and in another breath with our mathematics master, and so find ourselves describing a sprint in terms of numerators and denominators and of relations between fractions in terms of efforts and despairs.

IV

PLEASURE

THE two specimens of logical litigation that we have so far
considered in detail, namely, the fatalist issue and Zeno's issue,
have been in a certain way academic dilemmas. We almost
deliberately *let* them worry us just because we found them intellectually interesting. They were, up to a point, like riddles to
which we want to get the answers only because getting the
answers is good exercise. From now on I want to discuss issues
which are more than riddles, issues, namely, which interest us
because they worry us; not mere intellectual exercises but live
intellectual troubles. There is a further feature of these two
issues which will be missing from the ones we shall now be
considering. These two issues both come to a sharp edge, indeed
a cuttingly sharp edge. Are some things our fault or is nothing
our fault? Can some things be averted or can nothing be
averted? Does Achilles catch the tortoise at the second milestone or does he go on overtaking him asymptotically through
all eternity? But from now on we shall seldom or never be in
the simple if uncomfortable position of being pulled just from
North and South at once. We shall be in the complex and uncomfortable position of being pulled from a number of directions
at the same time.

In this lecture I am going to discuss a small and arbitrary
selection of questions about the notion or concept of pleasure.
But you will, I hope, realize from the start that these questions
will necessarily involve an expanding circle of other concepts.
Just as the wicket-keeper cannot keep wicket unless other
cricketers perform their cricketing-functions too, so the business
of such words as 'enjoy', 'like' and 'pleasure' is *ex officio*
meshed in with the variegated businesses of countless other
words.

Although the particular topic that I shall discuss here exemplifies some genuine dilemmas my motive in discussing it is not
only to draw attention to further specimens of dilemma.
In preparation for some matters that will occupy us later on,

I want to show one sort of source from which dilemmas can derive. I want, that is, to exhibit how, at the level of thought on which we have first to think not just *with* but *about* even a quite commonplace concept or family of concepts, it is natural and even inevitable for us to begin by trying to subject it to a code or standard, which we know how to operate elsewhere. Dilemmas result when the conduct of the new conscript diverges from the imposed standard. A well-tried control fails to control it. A child, hearing that an inspector from the Ministry of Agriculture and Fisheries was a Government official, might expect him to be a sort of policeman. He is well acquainted with some of the obvious functions of policemen. Only after finding him not doing what policemen do and doing what policemen do not do and so on, will he realize that inspectors from the Ministry of Agriculture are not any kind of policemen; nor yet are they postmen or coastguards or telephone-exchange operators. Somewhat so, we, at a higher level of abstraction, may come correctly to place a concept or family of concepts only after we have tried and failed to lodge it in some familiar framework of ideas—to stow it away, so to speak, in a chest of drawers that we regularly use, or to hang it on one of the hooks of the dresser where our cups and mugs have always gone.

The notions of *enjoying* and *disliking* are not technical notions. Everyone uses them, and there is no coterie of experts who, by dint of their special training or calling, are the ultimate authorities on their use. We know as a rule quite well, though without using any specialist methods of research, whether we enjoyed something or not this morning, and even, more generally, whether we prefer cricket to football. Nor do any logical embarrassments arise while we are making our everyday, ground-floor use of these familiar notions, that is, roughly, when we are not talking about pleasure, but about the games, wines or jokes that we have liked or disliked. In a certain use of the word 'about', a person who says that he used to enjoy reading Dickens more than Jane Austen, but now prefers her to him might properly deny that he was talking about pleasure. He was talking about the two novelists. He would want to say that he is not talking about pleasure until he starts to discuss such generalities as whether people should always put duty before pleasure or whether the fact that more people like the novels of Marie Corelli than like the novels of Jane Austen proves that the former are the better novels. Here he would be talking about pleasure, namely, in the one case discussing a moralist's question about the relations between duty and pleasure, in the other a literary critic's question about the relations between enjoyment and literary taste.

There are many overlapping fields of discourse in which, long before philosophizing begins, generalities about pleasure are bound to be mooted and debated. The moral educator in inculcating standards of conduct, the psychologist in trying to classify the springs of human action, the economist in correlating differences of price with difference in level of consumers' preferences, and the art-critic in comparing the appeals of different works of art, all must talk in general terms about, among many other things, the pleasure that human beings do or should take in different things. It is in the interplay of these and kindred generalities, of whose truth, when considered separately, we have no general doubts, that our characteristic problems arise.

I begin by considering a piece of theoretical harness which some pioneers in psychological theory, with natural over-confidence, formerly tried to hitch on to the notion of pleasure. Thinking of their scientific mission as that of duplicating for the world of mind what physicists had done for the world of matter, they looked for mental counterparts to the forces in terms of which dynamic explanations were given of the movements of bodies. Which introspectible phenomena would do for purposive human conduct what pressure, impact, friction and attraction do for the accelerations and decelerations of physical objects? Desire and pleasure, aversion and pain seemed admirably qualified to play the required parts; all the more so since it is common knowledge that normally people want what they will enjoy having when they get it, are normally glad to get what they had wanted to have, and when they choose between one thing and another, they prefer the thing they choose to the thing they reject. These states of mind are suitably variable in degree, as well as in duration. Something like the parallelogram of forces could be expected to apply to our competing and co-operating likes and dislikes, wants and aversions.

Hence it seemed reasonable to set up as axioms of human dynamics such plausible, yet also unplausible, propositions as that all desires are desires for pleasure; that all purposive actions are motivated by the desire for a net increase in the quantity of the agent's pleasure or a net decrease in the quantity of his pain; and that the dynamic efficacy of one pleasure differs from that of another only if the former is bigger, i.e. more intense or more protracted or both than the latter. It seemed an obvious, if unpalatable, deduction from these axioms that the altruist differs from the selfish man only in the fact that the altruist's self-indulgences happen to be of sorts which increase the pleasures of others. It is because it is a treat to him to give treats to others that he acts, as we incorrectly say, self-sacrificingly. Only the prospect of pleasure for himself can move him so to act.

This representation of pleasures as effects of acts, the desire for which effects is the cause of those acts, seemed to fit in well with the already prevalent grouping together of pleasure with pain. As wasp-stings hurt us, and as the fear of such hurts is what commonly prompts us to keep clear of wasps, so, but in the opposite direction, pleasures were construed as feelings engendered by actions and other happenings; and the desire to have these feelings was construed as being what prompts us to perform or secure the things which produce them; and as pains differ in duration and intensity and are the worse the longer they last and the more intense they are, so, according to this dynamic theory, pleasures had to be analogous feelings or sensations, capable of analogous quantitative variations. Indeed it was commonly assumed that pleasure stands to pain as hot to cold or as rapid to slow, i.e. it is what occupies the opposite end of the very same scale. The mensuration and calculation of amounts of pleasure will be just the obverse of the mensuration and calculation of amounts of pain. Plus quantities of the one are minus quantities of the other.

Now though we are, in effect, told by this kind of theory that the role of the concept of *pleasure* is the precise counterpart of the role of the concept of *pain*, as that of *north* is the counterpart of that of *south*, there are insuperable objections to playing them as proper counterparts. We are ready to say that some things hurt us, while others please or delight us; and ready to say that

some things give us pain, while others give us pleasure. But we
fight shy of saying, for example, that two minutes ago I had a
pain, and one minute ago I had a pleasure; or that while my
headache was the effect of eye-strain, my pleasure was the effect
of a joke or of the smell of a rose. We can tell the doctor where
it hurts and whether it is a throbbing, a stabbing or a burning
pain; but we cannot tell him, nor does he ask, where it pleases
us, or whether it is a pulsating or a steady pleasure. Most of
the questions which can be asked about aches, tickles and other
sensations or feelings cannot be asked about our likings and
dislikings, our enjoyings and detestings. In a word, pleasure is
not a sensation at all, and therefore not a sensation on one scale
with an ache or twinge.

Other considerations confirm this point. Some sensations, like
some tickles, are pleasant; others, like some other tickles, are
unpleasant. One scalding sensation may be distressing, when
the equally acute, scalding sensation given by a gulp of hot tea
may be pleasant. On rare occasions we are even ready to say
that something hurts, and yet we like it, or at least do not mind
it. If pleasure were correctly classified as a sensation, we should
expect it to be possible correspondingly to describe some of these
sensations, too, as pleasant, some as neutral and others as unpleasant, and yet this palpably will not do. The two last would
be contradictions, the first either a redundancy or worse. If I
have been enjoying a game, there need not have been something
else in progress, additional to the game, which I also disliked or
enjoyed, namely some special sensation or feeling engendered in
me by the game.

A person whose foot is being hurt by a tight shoe or whose
finger is being tickled by a butterfly may attend to the pain or
tickle without thinking at all about what is causing the sensation; or he may be thinking about the shoe or the butterfly without paying any heed at all to the pain or the tickle. Not only may
something be hurting or tickling him without his knowing what
it is that is doing so, but also he can be so absorbed in something
else that for a time he totally forgets his pain or tickle as well
as what causes it. But enjoyment and dislike are related to heed
and knowledge in entirely different ways. It is impossible, not
psychologically but logically impossible, for a person to be

enjoying the music while paying no heed at all to it, or to be detesting the wind and sleet while completely absorbed in quarrelling with his companion. There is a sort of contradiction in describing someone as absent-mindedly enjoying or disliking something.

Nor can he conceivably require to be told what it is that he is enjoying or disliking, save that he may be glad to have the delightful smell identified for him or to have described just what it was in her tone of voice that he did not care for. Pleasure and distaste do not require diagnosis in the ways in which sensations may very well require it. The fact that I have come to like some things and dislike others has an explanation and of this explanation I may or may not be ignorant. But when I have just been amused by some particular joke, the question 'What gave me that pleasure?' does not await an answer. For of course I already know that it was that joke, if it was that joke that had amused me.

In the way in which a sensation or feeling is a predecessor, a concomitant, or a successor of other happenings, enjoyment is not a predecessor, concomitant or successor of anything. My foot may hurt, continuously or intermittently, both while the shoe is on and after it is removed. The pressure on the sore toe and the pain it gives can be separately clocked. But when I enjoy or dislike a conversation, there is not, besides the easily clockable stretches of the conversation, something else, stretches of which might be separately clocked, some continuous or intermittent introspectible phenomenon which is the agreeableness or disagreeableness of the conversation to me. I might indeed enjoy the first five minutes and the last three minutes of the conversation, detest one intermediate stage of it and not care one way or the other about another stage. But if asked to compare in retrospect the durations of my enjoyings and dislikings with the durations of the stretches of the conversation which I had enjoyed or disliked, I should not be able to think of two things whose durations were to be compared. Nor can my pleasure in contributing and listening to the conversation be some collateral activity or experience which might conceivably clamour for a part of my interest or attention, in the way in which a tickle might distract my attention from the butterfly.

It is more nearly correct to say that my liking and disliking are not special objects of a possible secondary, introspective interest but rather special qualities of my actual interest in the conversation; and that this interest itself is not a concomitant of my active and receptive conversational activities, but is the special quality of those activities themselves.

It may be thought that it is after all a venial and unimportant fault to misclassify pleasure with sensations. No great harm is done, in ordinary circumstances, if we misclassify rabbits as a species of rat or sweet-peas as a species of Umbelliferae. But ours is a different sort of misclassification. It is not a case of trying to play a conceptual salmon with a conceptual trout-rod instead of with the correct salmon-rod; it is a case of trying to play a conceptual salmon with a cricket-bat or an ace of spades.

Much more important consequences follow. The assimilation of liking and disliking to sensations was only an item of the general programme of constructing a dynamic theory of human conduct, in which theory such things as wantings and likings were to provide the mental counterparts to the pressures, impacts, frictions and attractions of mechanical theory. Psychic motions would become calculable when the durations and intensities of desires and pleasures became measurable or estimable and when the compositions of complexes of these forces could be analysed into their components. A pleasure must be something having a determinate magnitude, at least in duration and intensity. It must be a process, on all fours with the process of something applying friction to something. But our objections to classifying pleasure with sensations had the quite general effect, if I am not wrong, of showing that pleasure is not a process of any sort. The concept of enjoying will not go through the logical hoops of processes. Processes are characterizable as relatively fast or slow, but, as Aristotle saw, I cannot enjoy something quickly or slowly. Whatever may be the place, and it is certainly an important place, of the notions of liking and disliking in the description of human conduct, it is not the place required for them by the projected dynamic theory. It is no good saying that this pony ought to fit that harness or must be refashioned in order to fit it. It was the wrong harness, and must be scrapped or used elsewhere.

An even more general point may be made. Pains are the
effects of such things as the pressure of a shoe on a toe, and they
are the causes of such things as winces. The idea of the projected
dynamic theory of human conduct was that pleasure should in
the same way be what causes some things, namely human
actions, and be the effect of other things, so that there might be
causal regularities of the patterns 'Whenever so and so, then
a pleasure' and 'whenever a pleasure, then such and such'. (The
awkwardness of such dictions itself signals some logical misfit.)

A pleasure, it was assumed, has got to be a recordable occurrence, in the way in which a flash of lightning and a clap of
thunder are recordable occurrences, if the propositions of the
desired science of human nature are to have the officially prescribed shape. We need not pause here to query the credentials
of this doctrine that all or the best scientific statements are of the
venerated 'lightning-thunder' shape. What is wanted is to
realize that statements about our enjoyings and dislikings will
not, without logical violence, be transformed into statements of
the 'lightning-thunder' pattern. Where we can ask how long
was the interval between the flash and the bang, we cannot ask
how long was the interval between seeing the point of a joke and
enjoying it—and not because, like some thunder-claps which are
heard at the same moment as the lightning is seen, the seeing
and the enjoying of the joke were synchronous happenings, but
because there were not two happenings to be synchronous *or*
separate. Lightning and thunder are distinguishable phenomena,
whether synchronous or not. But the enjoyment and the seeing
of a joke are not in this way two different phenomena, even
though other things than jokes are enjoyed and even though
some jokes are seen but not enjoyed. Though thunder-claps
never do occur in the absence of lightning, we can conceive of
them doing so. We cannot conceive of enjoyment occurring on
its own. We could not make sense of the statement that someone
had been just enjoying, any more than we could of the statement
that he had been simply being interested or merely absorbed.
The verb 'enjoy' is a transitive verb, where the verbs 'thunder'
and 'rumble' are not.

If one knows anything of the history of hedonistic psychological theories and of hedonistic and utilitarian ethical theories,

one knows how, all along their fronts, there broke out local
fights between the champions of these theories and people who,
with or without other theories or dogmas to support them, were
antagonized by various corollaries and riders to these general
doctrines. People felt in their bones that it was one thing to
say, what everyone says, that, except in special circumstances,
what we do on purpose, we like rather than dislike doing, and
are glad rather than sorry to have done; and quite another to say
that in all purposive actions we are deliberately trying to secure
for ourselves the maximum quantity of the feeling of pleasure.
The former is a harmless truism, the latter sounds like a scientific
discovery, and one of a very disquieting sort. Again, it is a
harmless truism that unselfish and affectionate people like
bringing pleasure and happiness to others. But it seems a
demoralizing paradox to say that unselfish conduct is merely a
species of self-indulgent conduct, or that affectionate people are
merely people whose calculated treats to themselves happen to
require other people getting treats as well.

But we do not need to know anything about the history of
hedonistic or utilitarian theories in order to see the sorts of antagonisms that they provoke. For we ourselves have had our own
hedonistic and utilitarian moments, and felt our own disquiets
with them. We ourselves have felt, inarticulately enough, that
the ground-floor notions of liking and disliking which enter so
pervasively and yet so untendentiously into our everyday autobiographical and biographical reflections, have undergone some
subtle and suspect transformation when presented as the basic
forces which explain all of our choices and intentions. On the
other hand we ourselves have not only learned to think in terms
of hosts of proverbial, pedagogic, judicial, and homiletic
generalities about people's likes and dislikes, but have felt the
need to get these generalities organized together, in concert
with other affiliated generalities, perhaps into something like an
ethical code, perhaps into something like a psychological,
explanatory theory, perhaps into something like a theological or
religious scheme, or, more likely, into a loose association of all
of these together. Well though we know how to think auto-
biographically and biographically about people's enjoyments and
distastes, we do not come thereby to know well how to knit the

generalizations upon these thoughts into codes, theories or schemes. We do not, therefore, to start with possess the tools or the skills with which to correct or explode, for example, a suggested dynamic psychology which has taken so reputable a leaf out of so renowned a book as that of nineteenth-century physics. We are, rather, half-persuaded from the outset that what is declared in the *patois* of a scientific theory must itself be a scientific theory.

I might put this point, with a deliberate exaggeration, by saying that of course we all know how to conduct our everyday informative and argumentative businesses with the verbs 'enjoy', 'dislike' and 'hurt'; and yet we do not know how to conduct our businesses with such abstract nouns as 'pleasure', 'aversion' and 'pain', for all that the generalities expressed with the aid of these uncomfortable abstract nouns can be nothing but distillations of one sort or another out of what is conveyed with the help of those comfortable verbs. We know what sorts of things we can and cannot say about people liking and disliking things; but we do not necessarily also know what sorts of things we can and cannot say about pleasure. We do not talk in 'lightning-thunder' constructions of people liking and disliking things: but this does not save us from being persuaded by the theorist who says, in general terms and in a scientific tone of voice, that pleasure stands to what gives it as thunder stands to lightning, or as pain stands to scalding. For it is one thing to employ a concept efficiently, it is quite another to describe that employment; just as it is one thing to make proper use of coins and notes in marketing and quite another thing to talk coherent accountancy or economics. Efficiency at the one task is compatible with incompetence at the other, and a person who is not easily cheated when making purchases or getting small change, may easily be taken in by the wildest theories of exchange-values.

I want now briefly to sketch another way which has been attempted of fixing the role of the notion of pleasure in the description of human life and conduct. This second enterprise in conceptual harnessing, as I describe it, will probably have for you an old-fashioned, pre-scientific appearance. This is partly

why I choose to consider it, since not all intellectual schemes are
or pretend to be scientific theories. But I choose to consider it
for another reason as well, namely that this old-fashioned conceptual apparatus still has its attractions. Even sophisticated
people like ourselves relapse into the use of it and put some
reliance on it.

The problem in what sorts of terms human nature is to be
described was at one time thought to be solved or half-solved by
deliberately borrowing the idioms of politics. The institutions,
practices and classes of a developed Greek or Roman political
community were necessarily describable things, since its states-
men, judges, advocates, envoys and administrative officials had
to communicate to the public their advice, rulings, information
and decisions about those subjects. The language of politics is
a well-developed language, and much though not all of it
becomes a part of the language of nearly every citizen of the
community. It is not the private code of a privileged coterie.
Now it can for a variety of reasons be convenient and helpful to
talk of the constitution of a human being in political language.
As the assembly or the parliament of a community deliberates,
disputes and decides, so each of us by himself deliberates, disputes and decides. As laws can be disobeyed, and public
deliberations be interrupted or degenerate into squabbles between factions, so we individuals harbour our own private law-
breakers and our own private juntas. To the unruly mob in a
State there correspond potentially subversive elements in ourselves requiring always discipline and sometimes repression.
Self-command here is what government of the governed is there.
In particular, it seems appropriate to liken such things as terror,
wrath, greed, indolence and envy to the rioters, the rebels and
the *canaille* of a society. A person who is in the grip of such
passions as these is like a community in which law and order are
in abeyance. A furious or panic-stricken man cannot listen to the
voice of reason. He cannot think straight or heed the counsels of
those who can. Passion is in charge. Government has given way
to mob-rule. The man, like a State, is divided against himself.

This parallel strikes us nowadays as not much more than a
striking and picturesque metaphor. We should be somewhat
surprised to hear it drawn and developed even in a sermon, but

we should be greatly surprised to find it being used as the theoretical backbone of a book on psychology. For we have had two hundred years of psychological theories, the plots of which have been borrowed from mechanics, chemistry and, more recently, biology. We have also had nearly two thousand years of a religious and theological scheme of ideas, the theoretical plot of which, while certainly not drawn from any science, has not been drawn either from any set of Greek or Roman political and legal ideas.

None the less we continue to have our Platonic moments—moments, indeed, in which it seems much less outrageously far-fetched to describe a man whose anger is out of control by analogy with an *émeute* in a State than by analogy with, say, a non-equilibrium between two forces. In particular our moral counsels are better suited by the tones of voice of political orations than by the tones of voice of mechanical explanations.

We need not trouble ourselves here to look for unpicturesque paraphrases for the representations of control and loss of control of fury and terror in terms of the maintenance and breakdown of law and order. My immediate point is that this representation itself failed to allocate a suitable political niche for pleasure. If, to revive a now rather old-fashioned word, we give the title of 'passions' to the potentially subversive agencies in a man, namely terror, fury, mirth, hatred, disgust, despair and exultation, then to enjoy or dislike something is not to be the victim of a passion. Terror, fury and mirth can be paroxysms or frenzies. A person in such a state has, for the time being, lost his head or been swept off his feet. If a person is perfectly collected in his deliberations and movements, he cannot, logically cannot, be described as furious, revolted or in a panic. Some degree of temporary craziness is, by implicit definition, an internal feature of passion, in this sense of 'passion'. But no such connotations attach to pleasure—though they do, of course, to such conditions as thrills, transports, raptures and convulsions. If a participant in a discussion or a game greatly enjoys the discussion or game, he is not thereby estopped from having his wits about him. Else the keener a person was on golf or playing the fiddle the less would be he capable of doing these things intelligently. If to enjoy a thing in some degree were to be in that degree beside oneself, one would be distraught throughout the prosecution of all one's favourite occupations. Complete absorption in something would entail complete inability to think what one was doing; and this is absurd. Complete calmness does not exclude great pleasure. The concept of enjoyment refuses to go through the same logical hoops as fury, despair, panic or glee. It is not even a mild transport, for it is not a transport at all. Enjoyment is not something that we curb or fail to curb, repress or fail to repress, control or fail to control. If we try, whether whole-heartedly or half-heartedly, to spell out the constitution of the human microcosm against the larger letters of a political macrocosm, we may be able to read some of the relations between governors and governed in some of the relations between the individual's deliberations and his passions. But his likings and dislikings are not replicas in miniature of any of the elements of that political fabric. Our conceptual pony fits this borrowed harness as badly as it fitted the borrowed harness of nineteenth-century psychological dynamics.

But we must not be ungrateful to either of these borrowed trappings. We learn the powers of a borrowed tool side by side with learning its limitations, and we find out the properties of the material as well when we find out how and why the borrowed tool is ineffectual upon it, as when we find out how and why it is effectual. In the end we design the tool for the material—in the end, but never in the beginning. In the beginning we have still to find out the first things about the ways in which the material is and is not workable; and we explore it by trying out implements with which we have already learned to work other materials. There is no other way to start.

The notion of pleasure has in our own day ceased to be the topic of heated controversies—though not, in my opinion, for the reason that philosophers, preachers, psychologists, economists and educators have at last got its logical role agreed. They have, I guess, dropped the subject, because the nineteenth-century thinkers ran it to death. It was employed as their shared maid-of-all-work, who always bungled the tasks for which doctrinaires pronounced her to have the proper qualifications.

To pick up a thread that I left loose at an earlier stage, we can say that the concepts of enjoying and disliking have been wrongly alleged to be of the same category with having a pain; of the same category with the kinds of occurrences which rank as causes and effects of other occurrences; and of the same category with the passions of terror, disappointment, loathing or glee. To say this is just to give the general promise that there will be found ways in which the concepts of enjoying and disliking resist attempts to give to them even rough parity of discursive manipulation with the concepts of these other families. The logical disciplines which control these others fail to control them. Dilemmas derive from wrongly imputed parities of reasoning. Most of the questions about a person which would be answered, truly or falsely, by statements about his sensations, or, what are quite different, by statements about his transports, fits or storms, would not be answerable, falsely or truly, by statements about his likings and dislikings; and vice versa. The wicket-keeper neither revokes nor follows suit; he neither buys nor sells; he neither convicts nor lets off with a caution. He is in another line of business.

V

THE WORLD OF SCIENCE AND THE EVERYDAY WORLD

So far I have been trying to exhibit some of the features which are apt to characterize litigations between non-rival theories or lines of thought by examining some rather special and localized issues. You will have felt, I expect and hope, that the fatalist dilemma, Zeno's dilemma, and my puzzles about pleasure are all, though in different ways, somewhat peripheral or marginal tangles—tangles whose unravelling does not promise by itself to lead to the unravelling of the tangles that really matter, save in so far as it may be instructive by example. Henceforward I shall be discussing a spider's-web of logical troubles which is not away in a corner of the room, but out in the middle of the room. This is the notorious trouble about the relations between the World of Science and the Everyday World.

We often worry ourselves about the relations between what we call 'the world of science' and 'the world of real life' or 'the world of common sense'. Sometimes we are even encouraged to worry about the relations between 'the desk of physics' and the desk on which we write.

When we are in a certain intellectual mood, we seem to find clashes between the things that scientists tell us about our furniture, clothes and limbs and the things that we tell about them. We are apt to express these felt rivalries by saying that the world whose parts and members are described by scientists is different from the world whose parts and members we describe ourselves, and yet, since there can be only one world, one of these seeming worlds must be a dummy-world. Moreover, as no one nowadays is hardy enough to say 'Bo' to science, it must be the world that we ourselves describe which is the dummy-world. Before directly confronting this issue, let me remind you of a partly parallel issue which, though it exercised our great-grandfathers and grandfathers, does not any longer seriously exercise us.

When Economics was entering its adolescence as a science, thinking people were apt to feel themselves torn between two rival accounts of Man. According to the new, tough-minded account presented by the economists, Man was a creature actuated only by considerations of gain and loss—or at least he was this in so far as he was enlightened. The conduct of his life, or at least of his rational life, was governed by the principles of Supply and Demand, Diminishing Returns, Gresham's law and a few others. But Man as thus depicted seemed to be disastrously different from Man as depicted by the preacher, the biographer, the wife or the man himself. Which, then, was the real man and which the dummy-man, the Economic Man or the Everyday Man?

The choice was a hard one. How could one vote against the Economic Man without taking sides with the unscientific against the scientific story? There seemed to be a deadly rivalry between what economists said about the motives and policies of human beings and what ordinary people said about the motives and policies of the people with whom they lived—and it was the latter story that seemed doomed to be condemned. The brother, whom I ordinarily describe as hospitable, devoted to his branch of learning, and unexcited about his bank-balance, must be a dummy-brother if I am to take science seriously. My real brother, my Economic Brother, is concerned only to maximize his gains and minimize his losses. Those of his efforts and out-lays which do not pay are done in ignorance of the state of the market or else from stupidity in making his calculations about it.

We have, I think, outgrown this feeling that our grandparents had, that we have to choose between the Economic Brother and the brother whom we know. We no longer think or are even tempted to imagine that what the economist says about the marketings of men who want to minimize losses and maximize gains is a general diagnosis of people's motives and intentions. We realize that there is no incompatibility between (1) saying that my brother is not much interested in exchange-transactions, and (2) saying that if and when he is engaged in such a trans-action with the intention of trying to come out of it as well as possible, then he does, other things being equal, choose the cheaper of two otherwise similar articles and invest his savings where risks of loss are relatively slight and prospects of dividends are relatively good. This means that we no longer suppose that the economist is offering a characterization or even a mis-characterization of my brother or of anyone else's brother. He is doing something quite different. He is offering an account of certain marketing-tendencies, which applies to or covers my brother in so far as he concerns himself in marketing matters. But it does not say that he must or does often or does ever concern himself in such matters. In fact it does not mention him at all. Certainly it talks about the Consumer, or it talks about the Tenant, or the Investor, or the Employee. But in an important way this anonymous character is neither my brother nor *not* my brother but someone else's brother. He has not got a surname, though people who have got surnames often are, among thousands of other things that they are, consumers, investors, tenants and employees. In one way the economist is not talking about my brother or anyone else's brother at all. He does not know or need to know that I have a brother, or what kind of a man he is. Nothing that the economist says would require to be changed if my brother's character or mode of life changed. Yet in another way the economist certainly is talking about my brother, since he is talking about anyone, whoever he may be and whatever he may be like, who makes purchases, invests his savings or earns a wage or salary, and my brother does or might fill these bills.

Æsop told a story of a dog who dropped his bone in order to secure the tempting reflection of the bone. No child thinks that this was meant to be just an anecdote about a real dog. It was meant to convey a lesson about human beings. But which human beings? Hitler perhaps. Yet Æsop did not know that there was going to be a Hitler. Well, about Everyman. But there is no such person as Everyman. Æsop's story was, in one way, about Hitler or about anyone else you choose to name. In another way it was not about any person that you can name. When we are clear about these different ways in which a person is and is not what a moral or economic statement is about, we cease to think either that my brother is a well-camouflaged Economic Man or that the economist is asking us to believe in fables. The mortal conflict which our grandfathers felt to exist between economics and real life no longer bothers us very much

—at least until we become edified enough to think not about our brothers, but about the Capitalist and the Worker. They, of course, are quite different from people's brothers.

But we have not, I think, outgrown the feeling that there is a feud between the world of physical science and the world of real life, and that one of these worlds, presumably, sad to say, the familiar one, is a dummy. I want to persuade you that this notion is the product of an influential variety of cross-purposes between theories, and to show you some of the sources of these cross-purposes.

As a preface to the serious part of the argument I want to deflate two over-inflated ideas, from which derives not the cogency but some of the persuasiveness of the argument for the irreconcilability of the world of science with the everyday world. One is the idea of *science*, the other that of *world*.

(*a*) There is no such animal as 'Science'. There are scores of sciences. Most of these sciences are such that acquaintance-ship with them or, what is even more captivating, hearsay knowledge about them has not the slightest tendency to make us contrast their world with the everyday world. Philology is a science, but not even popularizations of its discoveries would make anyone feel that the world of philology cannot be accom-modated by the world of familiar people, things and happenings. Let philologists discover everything discoverable about the structures and origins of the expressions that we use; yet their discoveries have no tendency to make us write off as mere dummies the expressions that we use and that philologists also use. The sole dividedness of mind that is induced in us by learning any of the lessons of philology is akin to that which we sometimes experience when told, say, that our old, familiar paper-weight was once an axe-head used by a prehistoric warrior. Something utterly ordinary becomes also, just for the moment, charged with history. A mere paper-weight becomes also, just for the moment, a death-dealing weapon. But that is all.

Nor do most of the other sciences give us the feeling that we live our daily lives in a bubble-world. Botanists, entomologists, meteorologists, and geologists do not seem to threaten the walls, floors and ceilings of our common dwelling-place. On the contrary, they seem to increase the quantity and improve the arrangement of its furniture. Nor even, as might be supposed, do all branches of physical science engender in us the idea that our everyday world is a dummy-world. The discoveries and theories of astronomers and astro-physicists may make us feel that the earth is very small, but only by making us feel that the heavens are very big. The gnawing suspicion that both the terrestrial and the super-terrestrial alike are merely painted stage-canvas is not begotten by even hearsay knowledge of the physics of the immense. It is not begotten, either, by hearsay knowledge of the physics of the middle-sized. The theory of the pendulum, the cannon-ball, the water-pump, the fulcrum, the balloon and the steam-engine does not by itself drive us to vote between the everyday world and the so-called world of science. Even the comparatively minute can be accommodated by us without theoretical heart-searchings in our everyday world. Pollen-grains, frost-crystals and bacteria, though revealed only through the microscope, do not by themselves make us doubt whether middle-sized and immense things may not belong where rainbows and mirages or even dreams belong. We always knew that there were things too small to be seen with the naked eye; the magnifying-glass and the microscope have surprised us not by establishing their existence but by disclosing their variety and, in some cases, their importance.

No, there are, I think, two branches of science which, especially when in collusion with one another, produce what I may describe as the 'poison-pen effect', the effect of half-persuading us that our best friends are really our worst enemies. One is the physical theory of the ultimate elements of matter; the other is that one wing of human physiology which investigates the mechanism and functioning of our organs of perception. I do not think it makes much difference to the issue whether these ultimate elements of matter are described as the Greek atomists described them or as the twentieth-century nuclear physicist describes them. Nor do I think that it makes much difference whether we consider old-fashioned guesses or recent conclusive discoveries about the mechanism of perception. The upsetting moral drawn by Epicurus, Galileo, Sydenham and Locke is precisely that drawn by Eddington, Sherrington and

Russell. The fact that this upsetting moral was once drawn from a piece of speculation and is now drawn from well-established scientific theory makes no difference. The moral drawn is not a piece of good science now, and it was not a piece of bad science then.

So the so-called world of science which, we gather, has the title to replace our everyday world is, I suggest, the world not of science in general but of atomic and sub-atomic physics in particular, enhanced by some slightly incongruous appendages borrowed from one branch of neuro-physiology.

(b) The other idea which needs prefatory deflation is that of *world*. When we hear that there is a grave disparity between our everyday world and the world of science or, a little more specifically, the world of one wing of physical science, it is difficult for us to shake off the impression that there are some physicists who by dint of their experiments, calculations and theorizing have qualified themselves to tell us everything that is really important about the cosmos, whatever that may be. Where theologians used to be the people to tell us about the creation and management of the cosmos, now these physicists are the experts—for all that in the articles and books that they write for their colleagues and pupils the word 'world' seldom occurs, and the grand word 'cosmos', I hope, never occurs. There is some risk of a purely verbal muddle here. We know that a lot of people are interested in poultry and would not be surprised to find in existence a periodical called 'The Poultry World'. Here the word 'world' is not used as theologians use it. It is a collective noun used to label together all matters pertaining to poultry-keeping. It could be paraphrased by 'field' or 'sphere of interest' or 'province'. In this use there could be no question of a vendetta between the poultry world and the Christian world, since, while 'world' could be paraphrased by 'cosmos' in the phrase 'Christian world', it could not be so paraphrased in the other.

It is obviously quite innocuous to speak of the physicist's world, if we do so in the way in which we speak of the poultry-keeper's world or the entertainment world. We could correspondingly speak of the bacteriologist's world and the marine zoologist's world. In this use there is no connotation of cosmic authority, for the word 'world' in this use does not mean '*the* world' or 'the cosmos'. On the contrary, it means the *department* of interests which physicists' interests constitute.

But this is not the whole story. For while there are hosts of interests, scientific, political, artistic, etc., from which the interests peculiar to physicists are distinguished, while, that is, there are hosts of provinces of interest, which are different from without being rivals of the physicist's province, there remains an important respect in which the subject-matters of fundamental physical theory do comprehend or cover the subject-matters of all the other natural sciences. The specimens collected by the marine biologist, though of no special interest to the physical theorist, are still, in an indirect way, specimens of what he is specially interested in. So too are the objects studied by the geologist, the mycologist and the philatelist. There is nothing that any natural scientist studies of which the truths of physics are not true; and from this it is tempting to infer that the physicist is therefore talking about everything, and so that he is, after all, talking about the cosmos. So, after all, the cosmos must be described only in his terms, and can only be misdescribed in the terms of any of these other more special sciences or, more glaringly, in theological terms, or most glaringly of all, in the terms of everyday conversation.

Let me remind you that just as a little while ago I was not finding fault with economic theory when I argued that it told neither lies nor the truth about my brother's character, so I am not now finding fault with the theories of physicists when I argue that they tell neither lies nor the truth about the world, in any awe-inspiring sense of 'the world'. Just as I then argued that economic theory, without mentioning my brother, told the truth about any marketing-transactions that he or anyone else might engage in, so I am now arguing that the truths of fundamental physical theory are, without mentioning the cosmos, truths about anything whatsoever in the world.

Least of all am I trying to expound or contribute to any scientific theory. I have not got the competence and, if I had, I hope that I would not have the inclination. My sole concern is to show how certain non-scientific morals seem to be but are not consequential upon a certain sort of scientific theory. I am questioning nothing that any scientist says on weekdays in his working tone of voice. But I certainly am questioning most of what a very few of them say in an edifying tone of voice on Sundays.

I am now going to try to bring out the underlying logical pattern of the view that the truths of physical theory leave no room for the truths of daily life, and this I do by means of a long-drawn out analogy with which I hope you will bear for some little time. An undergraduate member of a college is one day permitted to inspect the college accounts and to discuss them with the auditor. He hears that these accounts show how the college has fared during the year. 'You will find', he is told, 'that all the activities of the college are represented in these columns. Undergraduates are taught, and here are the tuition-fees that they pay. Their instructors teach, and here are the stipends that they receive. Games are played, and here are the figures; so much for rent of the ground, so much for the wages of the groundsman, and so on. Even your entertainments are recorded; here is what was paid out to the butchers, grocers and fruiterers, here are the kitchen-charges, and here is what you paid in your college battels.' At first the undergraduate is merely mildly interested. He allows that these columns give him a different sort of view of the life of the college from the patch-work-quilt of views that he had previously acquired from his own experiences of working in the library, playing football, dining with his friends, and the rest. But then under the influence of the auditor's grave and sober voice he suddenly begins to wonder. Here everything in the life of the college is systematic-ally marshalled and couched in terms which, though colourless, are precise, impersonal and susceptible of conclusive checking. To every plus there corresponds an equal and opposite minus; the entries are classified; the origins and destinations of all pay-ments are indicated. Moreover, a general conclusion is reached; the financial position of the college is exhibited and compared with its position in previous years. So is not this expert's way, perhaps, the right way in which to think of the life of the college, and the other muddled and emotionally charged ways to which he had been used the wrong ways?

At first in discomfort he wriggles and suggests 'May not these accounts give us just one part of the life of the college?

The chimney-sweep and the inspector of electricity-meters see their little corners of the activities of the college; but no one supposes that what they have to tell is more than a petty fragment of the whole story. Perhaps you, the auditor, are like them and see only a small part of what is going on.' But the auditor rejects this suggestion. 'No', he says, 'here are the payments to the chimney-sweep at so much per chimney swept, and here are the payments to the Electricity Board at so much a unit. Everybody's part in the college life, including my own, is down here in figures. There is nothing departmental in the college accounts. Everything is covered. What is more, the whole system of accountancy is uniform for all colleges and is, at least in general pattern, uniform for all businesses, government departments and town councils. No speculations or hypotheses are admitted; our results are lifted above the horizons of opinion and prejudice by the sublime Principle of Double Entry. These accounts tell the objective truth about the entire life of the whole college; the stories that you tell about it to your brothers and sisters are only picturesque travesties of the audited facts. They are only dreams. Here are the realities.' What is the undergraduate to reply? He cannot question the accuracy, comprehensiveness or exhaustiveness of the accounts. He cannot complain that they cover five or six sides of college life, but do not cover the other sixteen sides. All the sides that he can think of are indeed duly covered.

Perhaps he is acute enough to suspect that there has been some subtle trick played by this word 'covered'. The tuition he had received last term from the lecturer in Anglo-Saxon was indeed covered, yet the accounts were silent about what had been taught and the auditor betrayed no inquisitiveness about what progress the student had made. He, too, the undergraduate himself, had been covered in scores of sections of the accounts, as a recipient of an Exhibition, as a pupil of the lecturer in Anglo-Saxon and so on. He had been covered, but not characterized or mischaracterized. Nothing was said about him that would not have fitted a much taller Exhibitioner or a much less enthusiastic student of Anglo-Saxon. Nothing had been said about him personally at all. He has not been described, though he has been financially accounted for.

Take a special case. In one way the auditor is very much interested in the books that the librarian buys for the college library. They must be scrupulously accounted for, the price paid for each must be entered, the fact of the actual receipt of the book must be recorded. But in another way the auditor need not be at all interested in these books, since he need not have any idea what the books contain or whether anybody reads them. For him the book is merely what is indicated by the price mark on its jacket. For him the differences between one book and another are differences in shillings. The figures in the section devoted to library accounts do indeed cover every one of the actual books bought; yet nothing in these figures would have been different had these books been different in subject-matter, language, style and binding, so long as their prices were the same. The accounts tell neither lies nor the truth about the contents of any of the books. In the reviewer's sense of 'describe', they do not describe any of the books, though they scrupulously cover all of the books.

Which, now, is the real and which the bubble-book, the book read by the undergraduate or the book whose price is entered in the library-accounts? Clearly there is no answer. There are not two books, nor yet one real book, side by side with another bubble-book—the latter, queerly, being the one that is useful for examinations. There is just a book available for students, and an entry in the accounts specifying what the college paid for it. There could have been no such entry had there not been the book. There could not be a library stocked with mere book-prices; though also there could not be a well-conducted college which had a library full of books but required no library accounts to be kept.

The library used by the student is the same library as that accounted for by the accountant. What the student finds in the library is what the accountant tells the pounds, shillings and pence of. I am suggesting, you see, that it is in partially the same way that the world of the philologist, the marine-biologist, the astronomer and the housewife is the same world as that of the physicist; and what the pedestrian and the bacteriologist find in the world is what the physicist tells him about in his double-entry notation.

I do not want to press the analogy beyond a certain point.

I am not arguing that a scientific theory is in all or many respects like a balance-sheet, but only that it is like a balance-sheet in one important respect namely that the formulae of the one and the financial entries of the other are constitutionally speechless about certain sorts of matters, just because they are *ex officio* explicit about other, but connected matters. Everything that the student says about the books in the library may be true, and everything that the accountant says about them may be true. The student's information about the books is greatly unlike the accountant's, and neither is it deducible from the accountant's information, nor vice versa. Yet the student's information is covered, in an important way, by the accounts, although these are constitutionally speechless about the literary and scholarly qualities of books which are just what interest the student. The appearance of a vendetta between the different ways of describing the library is as delusive an appearance as was the appearance of a vendetta between my way of talking about my brother and the economist's way of talking about anybody's brother. For though the accountant is, in some very general sense, telling the college about the books in the library, he is not, in the reviewer's sense of the word, describing or, of course, misdescribing these books at all. He is exhibiting the arithmetical relations holding during the financial year between the total bills paid to the booksellers for books and, somewhat indirectly, the total bills paid to the college for the use of those books. That there are such bills to record and, consequently, such arithmetical relations between their totals, itself logically presupposes that there are books in the library, actually bought from booksellers and actually available for reading by students. It logically presupposes that there are things of which the student's descriptions are either true or false, though these descriptions cannot be read out of the library accounts. Not only can the full history of the life of the college during the year accommodate both of these kinds of information about the books, but it could not include a page for either kind without having a page for the other. It is not a question of two rival libraries, or of two rival descriptions of one library, but of two different but complementary ways of giving information of very different sorts about the one library.

Popularizers of physical theories sometimes try to make us feel at home in their theories by saying that these theories tell us about chairs and tables. This does make us feel comfortable, just for the moment. But only for the moment, since in the next breath we hear that what these theories have to say about chairs and tables is totally unlike what we say about them to the parlourmaid and what the joiner says about them to us. Worse still, we are given the impression that what we and the joiner say about them is unscientific and will not do, while what they say about them is scientific and has got to do. In fact, of course, physical theorists do not describe chairs and tables at all, any more than the accountant describes the books bought for the library. The accountant talks about book-bills and so refers indirectly to the books paid for. But this indirect reference is not a description; nor therefore a description which vies for acceptance with the student's description; and not therefore a description the correctness of which involves the incorrectness of the student's description. What is true or false of book-bills is not true or false of books, or vice versa, and yet the fact that one statement is true of the book-bills itself requires that there are the other quite different statements which are true of the books. The corresponding thing holds in the other field. A bit of the theory of ultimate particles has no place in it for a description or misdescription of chairs and tables, and a description of chairs and tables has no place in it for a description or misdescription of ultimate particles. A statement that is true *or* false of the one is *neither* true *nor* false of the other. It cannot therefore be a rival of the other. The very fact that some statement in physical theory is true requires that some statement or other (it cannot be deduced which), about such things as chairs and tables are true.

A popularizing accountant might try to make us feel at home in his parallel columns by saying that a certain entry contained the audited truth about books. If successful, he might get us to feel that books have suddenly been deprived of their readable contents and become pale shadows of book-bills. One cannot say 'Bo' to accountancy, but one can and should say 'Bo' to the accountant who leaves his ledgers to edify us with the moral he pretends to draw from his accounts, namely that books are nothing but entries in columns of pounds, shillings and pence.

I hope that this protracted analogy has satisfied you at least that there is a genuine logical door open for us; that at least there is no general logical objection to saying that physical theory, while it covers the things that the more special sciences explore and the ordinary observer describes, still does not put up a rival description of them; and even that for it to be true in its way, there must be descriptions of these other kinds which are true in their quite different way or ways. It need not be a matter of rival worlds of which one has to be a bubble-world, nor yet a matter of different sectors or provinces of one world, such that what is true of one sector is false of the other.

In the way in which a landscape-painter paints a good or bad picture of a range of hills, the geologist does not paint a rival picture, good or bad, of those hills, though what he tells us the geology of are the same hills that the painter depicts or mis-depicts. The painter is not doing bad geology and the geologist is not doing good or bad landscape painting. In the way in which the joiner tells us what a piece of furniture is like and gets his description right or wrong (no matter whether he is talking about its colour, the wood it is made of, its style, carpentry or period), the nuclear physicist does not proffer a competing description, right or wrong, though what he tells us the nuclear physics of covers what the joiner describes. They are not giving conflicting answers to the same questions or to the same sort of question, though the physicist's questions are, in a rather artificial sense of 'about', about what the joiner gives his information about. The physicist does not mention the furniture; what he does mention are, so to speak, bills for such goods as, *inter alia*, bits of furniture.

Part of this point is sometimes expressed in this way. As the painter in oils on one side of the mountain and the painter in water-colours on the other side of the mountain produce very different pictures, which may still be excellent pictures of the same mountain, so the nuclear physicist, the theologian, the historian, the lyric poet and the man in the street produce very different, yet compatible and even complementary pictures of one and the same 'world'. But this analogy is perilous. It is risky enough to say that the accountant and the reviewer both give descriptions of the same book, since in the natural sense of 'describe' in which the reviewer does describe or misdescribe the book, the accountant does neither. But it is far riskier to characterize the physicist, the theologian, the historian, the poet and the man in the street as all alike producing 'pictures', whether of the same object or of different objects. The highly concrete word 'picture' smothers the enormous differences between the businesses of the scientist, historian, poet and theologian even worse than the relatively abstract word 'description' smothers the big differences between the businesses of the accountant and the reviewer. It is just these smothered differences which need to be brought out into the open. If the seeming feuds between science and theology or between fundamental physics and common knowledge are to be dissolved at all, their dissolution can come not from making the polite compromise that both parties are really artists of a sort working from different points of view and with different sketching materials, but only from drawing uncompromising contrasts between their businesses. To satisfy the tobacconist and the tennis-coach that there need be no professional antagonisms between them, it is not necessary or expedient to pretend that they are really fellow-workers in some joint but unobvious missionary enterprise. It is better policy to remind them how different and independent their trades actually are. Indeed, this smothering effect of using notions like *depicting*, *describing*, *explaining*, and others to cover highly disparate things reinforces other tendencies to assimilate the dissimilar and unsuspiciously to impute just those parities of reasoning, the unreality of which engenders dilemmas.

But you will not and should not be satisfied with this mere promise of a lifebelt. Can it be actually produced and thrown to us in the precise stretch of surf where we are in difficulties? To one particular place where the surf is boiling round us I shall now turn.

VI

TECHNICAL AND UNTECHNICAL CONCEPTS

GALILEO, whose lead was quickly followed by Descartes and Newton, showed that a scientific theory has no place in it for terms which cannot appear among the data or the results of calculations. But colours, tastes, smells, noises and felt warmth and cold cannot, it seems, appear there. So there is no place for them in scientific theories. What the thermometer records has its place there, but not what the fingers or the lips register; the frequencies and amplitudes of the vibrations propagated through air, but not the notes that constitute heard melodies. To us it makes a big difference whether we are blind, colour-blind, or dazzled, and whether we look at things in sunlight or moonlight, through white glass or tinted glass; but the facts about light recorded and organized in the theory of optics are indifferent to these personal differences to us. The chemist, the geneticist and the wielder of the Geiger counter, in apparent defiance of this ostracism of sensible qualities, may indeed base their special theories on the smells and tastes of chemical compounds, on the colours of sweet-peas and on the clicks heard from the Geiger counter, but this does not suffice to reinstate these sensible qualities in the aristocracy of genuine physical facts. It shows only that they can, in certain conditions and when plenty of precautions are taken, be a reliable index to these facts, somewhat, perhaps, as a stomach-ache can be a reliable index to the presence of strychnine in the food consumed, though the food did not and could not incorporate any stomach-aches. Since scientific truths are about what can carry and be carried by calculations, colours, tastes and smells which cannot be so carried must belong not to the facts of physics, but elsewhere, namely either to the facts of human and animal physiology or to the facts of human and animal psychology. Colours are either in the eye of the beholder or else in the mind of the beholder. They are his rejected gift to the world. Here and here only can the iridescences of the bubble enjoy their slippery existence.

This doctrine has had a great influence and there is something in it which is true and important. It brings out into the open a fundamental logical property of the formulae that can be ingredients in an exact scientific theory. But we need to notice one or two possible traps. First, even if it is true that physical theory cannot accommodate mentions of the colours or tastes of things, this does not by itself prove that mentions of the colours and tastes of things are to be construed as mentions of things existing or happening in people's physiological or psychological insides. Certainly our insides are always a convenient limbo in which to bundle our miscellanea. The human mind in particular is traditionally the 'Pending' tray for theorists' unanswered letters. But so far as the argument has yet gone, it need not be the right tray. That it is the right tray follows, or seems to follow, only from some further, much more specific arguments, some of which we shall consider later.

Next, the fact that mentions of colours and tastes cannot occur in the formulae of physical theory does not by itself prove that these formulae may not *cover* or *apply to*, without *describing*, just those things the describing of which requires the mention of colours and tastes. You cannot get mentions of the brands or the origins of wines into the arithmetic of the pipes, gallons and pints of wine for which ship-space is wanted by the shipper. For him the differences between two gallons of red, vintage wine and five gallons of cheap, white wine is three gallons, *sans phrase*. Yet the gallons to be shipped cannot conceivably be mere gallons *sans phrase*; they are, for example, gallons of wine, and of wine with discoverable chemical as well as dinner-table properties. It is not true that what is not and cannot be mentioned in a formula is denied by that formula. If a supercargo's quota of cubic feet in the hold is given, for example, a vintner's implementation, then it is capable of that implementation among others. What it is not capable of is unimplementability. A public car-park need not have in it this or that particular car, or any cars of this or that make, or even any cars at all. But one thing it must have, and that is *room* for cars, no matter whose and no matter of which makes. The one thing it cannot have is a barrier against the entry of cars. It is not because it is totally inhospitable but because it is totally hospitable, that its notice-

boards are silent about my and your car, and about Rolls Royces
and Morris Minors. Again, it is not because algebraical equa-
tions will have nothing to do with numbers, that they mention
none of them. Rather it is because they are impartially receptive
of any numbers you please. x is not a rival to 7, it is a hotel for
7 or for any other number. So the logically necessary silence of
physical formulae about mahogany and oak or about colours and
tastes need not be construed as proclaiming a shut door. It can
be construed instead as proclaiming a wide-open door. Precisely
this is the way that we had, I think, to construe the silence of the
college accounts about the contents of the books bought for its
library. Only book-prices were mentioned, but this restriction
was not merely compatible with the books that were bought for
these prices having other properties than these prices; it was
actually incompatible with books being nothing more than the
vehicles of purchase-prices. An object could not be merely something costing half-a-crown. The accounts were indeed entirely
silent about the literary and scholarly merits and demerits of the
books, but the silence was not a denial of the existence of any
such qualities but, so to speak, a declaration of total indif-
ference to which of these and other qualities belonged to which
of the books. Pounds, shillings and pence are common denominators, and common denominators cannot be exclusive.

It is worth while indicating one intellectual motive for what
I argue to be this error of construing a logically necessary
impartiality as a logically necessary hostility. The hold of
Aristotelian logic was, for both good and ill, very strong on
seventeenth- and eighteenth-century theorists. So it seemed to
be beyond question that the measurable dimensions of an object,
say its thermometer temperature or its speed in yards per
second, characterized it in the same general sort of way as its
colour or taste were naïvely supposed to do. It seemed natural
to list them both as Qualities. It then seemed necessary to draw
a line between the qualities which have to be mentioned and
operated with in physical theory and the qualities which cannot.
They were in fact so distinguished—first, I believe, by Boyle—
as the 'Primary' and 'Secondary Qualities' respectively. But
then the scientifically blue-blooded Primary Qualities could not
tolerate sharing a bench with the rude Secondary Qualities, and

these had, in consequence, to be deprived of their title to be qualities of things at all. Clearly the mistake was to put them on the same bench at the start, but Aristotle's economy in benches was not yet recognized to be a piece of personal stinginess. Perhaps even we have inherited something of this stinginess. For we are still able to be influenced by the argument that as the description of a table given by a physicist mentions and can mention nothing of what enters into the joiner's description, therefore the joiner's description must be abandoned. In letting this argument influence us, we are supposing that there is just one rather short bench for everything that we can call 'descriptions'; we are forgetting that, for example, what the economist says about the investor could be listed as a 'description' of my brother, despite the fact that since the economist cannot say what my brother is like or even that I have a brother he is in no position, besides having no call, to describe him, in the sense of 'describe' in which I am in a good position to describe him. The undiscriminating employment of smother-expressions, like 'Quality', 'Property', 'Predicate', 'Attribute', 'Characteristic', 'Description' and 'Picture' reinforces our other temptations to treat as like one another concepts which in their daily jobs do not work at all like one another. It is their refusals to play the parts assigned to them which constitute dilemmas.

What I want to do now is to bring out more clearly some ways in which different concepts, though applying to the same subjects, apply to them in very different manners. The parts they play are not rival parts.

Are the cards with which we play Poker the same as those with which we play Bridge or are they different? Certainly they are the same. But are the properties or attributes of the cards which the Poker-player notices or misses the same as those which the Bridge-player notices or misses? Do these players give the same descriptions of them, or different and even conflicting descriptions of them? This is not so easy to answer. For while both may notice that a certain card is the Queen of Hearts, one of them realizes, or perhaps fails to realize, that it is the last surviving trump-card, while the other has no such expression even, in his Poker-vocabulary. He realizes, on the contrary, or perhaps fails to realize, that it is the card which will complete his straight flush—an attribute of which the Bridge-player knows nothing. Well, is one of them right and the other wrong? Is the player who lists the card as a trump-card the victim of an illusion from which the Poker-player is exempt? Or is he, on the other hand, a specially acute observer or diagnostician, in contrast with the Poker-player who is put off with mere superficial appearances? Is the Poker-player, unhappily, trump-blind? Is the Queen of Hearts really, though not manifestly, endowed with the important property or attribute of being a trump-card; or is it just the Bridge-player's systematic delusion that this is so, since it is really, say, the completion of a straight flush? Or is it really neither of these things, but just a Queen of Hearts? Obviously this is not a genuine perplexity. The question whether this Queen of Hearts is, at a particular moment, a trump-card or not depends on the prior question whether four people are playing Bridge with the pack containing this card; and what makes Hearts, or some other suit, trumps is nothing occult or latent behind the glossy faces of the cards, but simply the general nature of the game of Bridge and the particular turn the bidding has taken during a particular stretch of the game.

The only perplexing thing in the situation is whether we ought to say that being a trump-card is a 'property' or 'attribute' of the Queen of Hearts. We know how to find out whether it is a trump or not, and we know what we can do with it if it is a trump that we cannot do with it if it is not. What is not so clear—and is also quite immaterial to the play—is whether or not we should classify this knowledge as knowledge of a 'property' or 'attribute' of the card. This is not a Bridge-player's worry but a logician's worry. The fact that this is an invented and frivolous worry even for logicians does not matter, since we shall see, I hope, that it is of a piece with some kindred worries which are not invented or frivolous.

The question what the Queen of Hearts can and cannot do cannot be answered at all unless we know the game in which it is being employed, and specific information about what she can and cannot do in a certain state of the game requires some specific knowledge about what has been going on since the last deal.

The corresponding thing is true at a more elementary level still. A child, who could recognize the card for a picture of a queen, oddly decorated with red heart-shaped patterns, might have as yet no idea how packs or suits of cards are composed, much less any idea that there are games the rules of which allot different values or powers to the different members of a suit. The notion that most often a Queen is 'higher' than a Jack but 'lower' than a King would not yet have dawned on him.

The rules of Bridge were man-invented and can be amended when we like. Nor need we play Bridge or any other game at all. But if Bridge is being played, then the question whether a given card is a trump-card or not is not itself conventional. We cannot then have it which way we like. It is not a matter of mere arbitrary dubbing. We can forget and be reminded what are trumps; we can make mistakes about what are trumps and be corrected or penalized; a spectator can infer correctly or incorrectly to what are trumps from the way the hands are played. It is an objective, public fact that a given card is a trump-card, though its being so is a matter of some highly arbitrary conventions being voluntarily conformed to and applied.

The same sorts of considerations apply to the familiar marketing-concepts which we employ when thinking about shopping. It is not difficult to see that while having such and such a market-price can be called a property or attribute of a commercial article, such logicians' appellations need to be hedged with the same sorts of precautions. There might not have been such a thing as money; there can be money where there are no pounds, shillings or pence; the purchasing power of pounds, shillings and pence can be modified by policy as well as from other causes; and retailers have some margin of freedom within which to fix the prices of their goods. None the less, in the context of the monetary system we have, the way it is working, and the retailer's decision, it is a public, objective fact that the commodity costs so many pounds, shillings and pence. We have to discover its price, and we cannot get a different price attached to it by private fiats. Moreover, where we can abstain from playing Bridge, we are bound to take part in the marketing-game—only, of course, for that very reason among others, it is not a game. Here too, there can be no question of the price of a commodity being construed as an invisible quality of the thing, whose detection requires some mysterious super-perceptive faculties or some abnormal diagnostic powers. We all know how to find out what things cost and we all know what is involved in their costing what they do. To know this we have merely to get the hang of an apparatus of financial and commercial terms, and to apply these to particular cases. It would be absurd to imagine, say, an Esquimau researcher, who had no monetary terminology and no grasp of simple arithmetic, finding or even looking for the prices of articles. It would be absurd, too, to doubt whether an article could both be worth 2s. 6d. and be palatable; or to ask which of these properties was a real and which a merely apparent property of the article. There could be no logical rivalry between them. They are not jealous applicants for seats on the same bench.

The thinking in which we operate with the terms or concepts of Bridge is considering how to win the game. The thinking in which we operate with the terms or concepts of commerce is considering how to make the best bargains. But the thinking in which we operate with the terms or concepts of a scientific theory is directed not towards victories or profits but towards knowledge. This gives us an extra and important motive for taking the terms of a scientific theory to stand for genuine qualities or properties of things. It also gives us a powerful inducement to overlook the numerous ways in which our operations with these terms is like our operations with the terms of Bridge and the terms of retail or wholesale trade. Where we are not seriously perplexed by the question whether behind the features of the Queen of Hearts which the child can see, there do not covertly reside some grander properties which he fails to detect, such as the card's being a trump-card, we can be seriously perplexed by the question whether behind the warmth of the bath-water which the child feels with his hand, there does not covertly reside some grander property which he fails to detect, namely the thermometer-temperature of the water.

Where no one, unless while taking part in logicians' debates, feels any inclination to ascribe greater or deeper reality to the price than to the taste of a loaf of bread, we all of us feel strongly inclined, in certain intellectual moods, to ascribe greater or deeper truth to a formula giving the chemical composition of the bread than to the baker's or the consumer's information about it. Here we feel a kind of logical rivalry; there we did not feel it, though we could, with our logical tongues in our cheeks build up the semblance of a case for there being such a rivalry. The case there was transparently hollow; the case here, even if hollow, is less transparently hollow.

Part of the general point that I am trying to make can be put in this way. Though phonetically and grammatically the phrase 'trump-card' is even shorter and simpler than the phrase 'Queen of Hearts', the concept of *trump-card* incorporates over and above the moderate complexities of that of *Queen of Hearts* or *three of Diamonds* all the extra complexities which constitute what we have to learn in order to be able to operate in games of Bridge with the term 'trump'. This huge difference in level of complexity is smothered if we very earnestly employ for concepts of the two very different levels the same umbrella-words 'property', 'quality' and 'attribute'. The even more hospitable umbrella-word 'concept' also helps to hide the differences between the heads that it covers. But even if we employ no such logicians' smother-words, we are still under some intellectual pressure to over-assimilate the complex and elaborate to the simple and manageable, or the not yet scheduled to the already scheduled. That is to say, when we are not at the moment playing Bridge, but standing back and considering Bridge terms and playing-card terms together, we can, in a way, momentarily forget what we know quite well while playing, and begin to wonder how truths of the one level tie in with truths of the other; to wonder, even, if assertions of the one level are not disqualified from being true by the truth of assertions of the other level. How, for instance, can a card which was a trump-card ten minutes ago, not be one now without having undergone a real change of intrinsic nature? Naturally in this particular field such moments are short and our wonderings only quarter-serious. For we can deliberately join a game and as deliberately leave it. It is our sport, we are not its sport. Its control over our thinking and acting is brief and easily rescinded. Moreover, it is only one of dozens of different sorts of card games. We can without intellectual embarrassment switch in a moment from

operating with the entire conceptual apparatus of Bridge to
operating with the entire conceptual apparatus of Poker or Old
Maid. There are no such rescindings or transfers of the controls
exercised over our thinking and acting by the conceptual
apparatus of established scientific theories. Here we have no
similar opportunities for, so to speak, standing on the platform
to wave 'good-bye for the present' to the departing team of
special concepts. We have no holiday from one another. Where
we can often and easily get a detached view of the sort of work
done, in its card-table setting, by a concept like *trump,* we cannot
often or easily get a detached view of the sort of work done by
a concept like *thermometer-temperature* or *Vitamin B.*

Influential too, is the fact that we can look up the codes of
Bridge which fix the roles of the concepts of Bridge; and we can
compare these codes word by word and phrase by phrase with
the codes of other games. We have no such manuals in which to
look up the codes which fix the roles of the concepts of a science,
or the concepts of untechnical life. We have to read the un-
written codes of their conduct out of their conduct and we have
no works of reference to tell us whether we have misread.

It is clear, I hope, how the meanings of the terms used by
Bridge-players and Poker-players are heavy with the systems or
schemes of those games. It would be absurd to suppose someone
learning what is meant by 'straight flush' without learning even
the rudiments of Poker, or learning all about Poker without
learning what a straight flush is. For brevity, let me describe
the term 'straight flush' as a 'Poker-laden' term. In the same
general sort of way the special terms of a science are more or
less heavy with the burthen of the theory of that science. The
technical terms of genetics are theory-laden, laden, that is, not
just with theoretical luggage of some sort or other but with the
luggage of genetic theory. Their meanings change with changes
in the theory. Knowing their meanings requires some grasp of
the theory.

So we can say, now, that it is relatively easy for an ordinary
Poker-player to explain in words the differences between the
quantity and type of luggage carried by an expression like
'straight flush' and the quantity and type of luggage carried by
an expression like 'Queen of Hearts'. But the corresponding

task in some other fields is far from easy. Precisely how much more theoretical luggage is carried by such a term as 'light-wave' than is carried by such a term as 'pink' or 'blue'? But at least one can discern very often that there is this important difference between one term and another, namely that one of them carries some of the luggage of a specific theory, while the other carries none from that theory, since, for example, the latter is properly handled by people who know nothing even of the rudiments of that theory. 'Queen of Hearts', for example, carries no Bridge-luggage. So at least in some important respects the terms peculiar to Bridge will be mismanaged if construed as being on an equal footing with terms which are not Bridge-laden. They cannot be treated as fellow-occupants of one bench, or as rivals for occupancy of one bench.

Our alarming and initially paralysing question was this. 'How is the World of Physics related to the Everyday World?' I have tried to reduce its terrors and dispel its paralysing effect, by asking you to reconstrue the question thus, 'How are the concepts of physical theory logically related to the concepts of everyday discourse?' I have asked you to see this question as having much in common with the questions 'How are the special terms of Bridge or Poker logically related to the terms in which the observant child describes the cards that are shown to him?' and 'How are the special terms of traders logically related to the terms in which we describe their commodities after we have brought them home?'

I shall not be surprised if you feel some impatience with the lengthy and somewhat factitious illustrations by which I have tried to disclose some of the kinds of difference in level and complexity between, for example, the concept of *trump* and that of *Queen of Hearts*, or between the concept of *thermometer-temperature* and that of *warmth*. I expect some of you to feel that I have or *ex officio* ought to have in my repertoire some neat, strict and systematized docketing-labels, by means of which I could just tell you, without relying on unreliable analogies, what the differences are between concepts and concepts, between, say, the technical concepts of a scientific theory and the semi-technical or untechnical concepts of the pavement. But I have no such packet of labels. They would do no good if I constructed a packet of them. The welter of technical concepts with which a scientist operates and the welter of untechnical and semi-technical concepts with which we all operate are welters not of homogeneous, but heterogeneous concepts. Even the relatively few technical terms of cricket or Bridge are highly variegated in kind.

But now I must move on to a certain very special tangle or tangle of tangles, which is, I think, for many people somewhere near the centre of their trouble about the relations between the World of Physical Science and the Everyday World. We can call this 'the Problem of Perception'. I shall not unravel the whole tangle, for the simple reason that I do not know how to do it. There are patches in it, and important ones where I feel like a bluebottle in a spider's web. I buzz but I do not get clear.

VII

PERCEPTION

How could anything be more familiar to us than seeing things, hearing things, smelling, tasting and touching things? We have our ordinary verbs of perceptual detection, discrimination and exploration under very good control long before we leave the nursery. Nor do we need to get much sophistication before we are pretty familiar with many of the more prevalent abnormalities of perception. We soon find out about seeing double, hearing the sounds of the sea in sea-shells, losing the senses of smell and taste; about rainbows, reflections and echoes; about magnifying glasses, mirrors and megaphones. We soon get the notions of blindness, deafness, numbness; of long sight, short sight and dazzlement; and having learned that these are connected with interference, damage or deficiency in the appropriate sense-organs, we are not surprised to find that spectacles make differences to what we see, but not to what we hear or taste, or that it is for the medical profession to find the causes of personal defects of perception and the remedies for them.

At the start we say and follow things said *with* verbs of perception where we are not yet talking *about* perceiving but about the things that we perceive or fail to perceive. At a later stage we learn, for example, to tell the oculist or ear-doctor the things that he wants to know, not facts about the clock we hear ticking or about the birds we see on the lawn, but facts about the way they sound and look to us. Already used to the idea that sometimes things are not as they look or sound to be, we soon get interested in such questions as why the distant bat sounds as if it strikes the ball quite a long time after it does strike, why the note of the engine's whistle drops as it passes us, and what makes the mountains look much nearer on some days than on others. We begin to talk about the conditions governing different classes of sights, felt temperatures and heard sounds.

There are hosts of notorious generalities about the limitations and fallibilities of our senses. The conjuror reminds us—of course in vain—that the quickness of the hand deceives the eye;

proverbs remind us that all that glitters is not gold; and Æsop's story of the greedy dog reminds us that the reflections of bones can be mistaken for bones until it comes to eating them.

Thinkers who wish to maintain the pre-eminence of mathematical knowledge over other beliefs, and thinkers who wish to depreciate mundane beliefs in favour of supra-mundane beliefs have often argued from these notorious facts of illusion, delusion and imprecision in sense-perception to the sweeping conclusion that we can never find out anything for certain by using our eyes, ears and noses. What is sometimes fraudulent may be always fraudulent. Where we have relied and been disappointed we should cease to rely. Even if there are some genuine articles, still they are stamped with no hall-marks. There is never anything to tell us that *this* is one of the genuine articles.

I do not want to spend long in examining the arguments for this general depreciation of sense-perception or the intellectual motives for denying all credentials to sense-perception in order to enhance those of calculation, demonstration or religious faith. I want to get quickly to the much thornier briar-patch, the place, namely, where scientific accounts of perception seem to issue in the consequential doctrine that observers, including the physiologists and psychologists themselves, never perceive what they naïvely suppose themselves to perceive. But as there is some cross-trading between the two firms, I must say a little about the quite general argument from the notorious limitations and fallibilities of our senses to the impossibility of our getting to know anything at all by looking, listening and touching.

A country which had no coinage would offer no scope to counterfeiters. There would be nothing for them to manufacture or pass counterfeits of. They could, if they wished, manufacture and give away decorated discs of brass or lead, which the public might be pleased to get. But these would not be false coins. There can be false coins only where there are coins made of the proper materials by the proper authorities.

In a country where there is a coinage, false coins can be manufactured and passed; and the counterfeiting might be so efficient that an ordinary citizen, unable to tell which were false and which were genuine coins, might become suspicious of the genuineness of any particular coin that he received. But however general his suspicions might be, there remains one proposition which he cannot entertain, the proposition, namely, that it is possible that all coins are counterfeits. For there must be an answer to the question 'Counterfeits of what?' Or a judge, who has found all too many witnesses in the past inaccurate and dishonest, may be right to expect today's testimonies to break down under examination; but he cannot declare that there are no such things as accuracy and sincerity in testifying. Even to consider whether this witness has been insincere or inaccurate involves considering what would be the honest or precise thing to say. Ice could not be thin if ice could not be thick.

But more than this. You and I know the general truth that we could be taken in by a counterfeit coin or a confidence-trickster; and in a particular contingency, though aware of the danger, we might still be without any conclusive or even worthwhile acid tests or lie-detectors by means of which to decide between the sham and the genuine. But our situation is not always like this. You and I sometimes make mistakes in counting, adding and multiplying, and we may remind ourselves of this general liability in the very same breath with making one of these mistakes. So, at first sight, it looks as though we ought to surrender and say that we can never find out by counting the number of chairs in a room and never find out by adding or multiplying the right answers to our arithmetical problems. Yet we do not surrender. For here we have in our possession all the acid tests and lie-detectors that we need. Namely we can count again, quite carefully, and compute again, quite carefully. Nor will this care be merely a useless, anxious watchfulness against nothing in particular. It will be vigilance for just those specific slips which we and our associates have made before and detected and corrected before. In this case we know by experience both what it is like to miscount and miscalculate and what it is like to avoid, detect and correct those miscalculations or miscountings. But still our precautions may not be sufficient. Perhaps we count three times, once fast and twice slowly, and not always starting in the same place; but still we miscount. Or perhaps we add, first going down from top to bottom, and then going up from bottom to top; but still we miscalculate. Very good—but how is the mistake exposed? By someone counting correctly or by someone adding correctly. The thing was doable; the thing was done. We did not do it, but we know all that went to the doing of it. We could have done it ourselves. So far from our thinking that perhaps nothing can ever be found out by counting or adding, we realize not only that things can be so found out but also that among the things that can be thus found out are mistakes in counting and adding.

Compare with these human fallibilities the fallibility of a proof-reader. He has to find the misprints, if any, on a printed page, and his only way of finding them, if they are there, is by seeing them. Perhaps he signals three and misses two. One of the three that he signals is not a misprint but an alternative legitimate spelling. He is told this and takes care not to make that mistake again, though this does not rule out all possibility of his making it again. What of the two misprints that he does find and the one that he misses? The two that he finds are there, and he found them by seeing them. So it was some good using his eyes. The one that he missed was, perhaps, found by someone else who found it by using his eyes. So it was some good his using his eyes too. Moreover, the proof-corrector himself admits in retrospect that he had overlooked that misprint, namely the misprint that he now sees when it is pointed out to him.

Using one's eyes is the only way of finding misprints and proof-readers with good or normal eyesight, who have had plenty of practice and who employ the techniques of their craft, can be relied on to find out nearly, though not quite all the misprints that are there to be found. The chances of mistakes and oversights never dwindle to nil; but they can and often do dwindle to negligible dimensions. But the proof-reader's candid confession 'It is always possible that I have missed a misprint' does not amount to the lament 'It is possible that I always miss all misprints', or to the despairing suggestion that perhaps everything printed in every book is misprinted, though quite undiscoverably misprinted.

For future purposes we should notice that while sometimes a proof-reader fails to see a misprint until it is pointed out to him, when he sees it well enough, sometimes he cannot see it even when it is pointed out to him—and there are different sorts of obstacles which prevent him from doing so. He cannot see misprints when he has a cataract; when the light is bad; when the page is several feet from his eyes. But also he may be unable to see it because he is flustered or hurried; or because he has not learned the language or the orthography of the misprinted word; or because he was himself the author of the passage and therefore knows so well what should be on the page that, without taking special precautions, he does not see that what is printed on the page is not what he meant to have there; or else he is thinking too much about the topic dealt with in the passage to think enough about how it is printed. He will reproach himself for having been the victim of some of these liabilities, but for others, like his cataract or the bad illumination, he will express regret but not remorse. That is, some of the explanations that he will give for some of his mistakes and failures will be of the same sort as the explanations he would give for his mistakes and failures in counting or multiplying, but some will be of quite different sorts, like the explanations that he couches in the terms of elementary ophthalmology or optics.

But even when his mistakes and failures are to be explained in ophthalmological or optical terms, this fact does not by itself prove the disheartening general proposition that nobody's eyes are ever any good for anything, with its tacitly implied rider that no proof-readers can really find out for certain whether there are misprints on a page or not. The existence of disabilities is evidence against and not in favour of the non-existence of abilities.

It makes all the difference whether the imputation of general fraudulence to the senses is made to rest on the existence of disabilities, like colour-blindness, or on the existence of inefficiencies in the exercises of our abilities. We can fail to spot misprints, though we see them quite well when they are pointed out to us; but so we can fail to detect fallacies in arguments, though we recognize them when they are pointed out to us. We can mistake a shadow for a snake, a mirage for a puddle, or a swarm of bees for a trail of smoke; but so we can give 54 as the product of 8 and 7. We can, but we need not. We know how not to make such mistakes, or if we do not yet know, we can still learn. We make these mistakes, not because there is anything wrong with our eyes but because we are still ignorant, or we are impetuous or indolent or the victims of rigid habits. We do not use our eyes as well as we might or as well as some other people do. Lapses of this kind are of a piece with lapses in counting, calculating, translating and reasoning. The fact that we can and often do go astray does not prove that we are forced astray, or that we cannot keep straight. On the contrary, we reprobate going astray by contrast with keeping straight and we only establish that someone has gone astray by going straight ourselves. Only paths that can be kept can be strayed from.

But the argument for the general fraudulence of the senses hinges, very often, not on the quite general facts that we are not always careful or always well educated, but on the much more special facts that our eyes, ears and noses are themselves subject to chronic or occasional impairments. It is not for want of trying or for want of training that the colour-blind cannot distinguish colours which the rest of us can distinguish. The fact that dogs can smell smells and hear shrill whistles which are out of our range reveals limitations in our equipment, not in our efficiency in using it. There certainly are hosts of facts of this general kind, many well known to everybody, many known only to specialists. But in so far as they go to show that there is much that we are not equipped to perceive, they do not, as yet, go any way towards showing that there is nothing that we are equipped to perceive. There are many things that are too big and many that are too small for me to handle with my hands or to chew with my teeth, but it does not follow and it is not true that I cannot handle pens or chew biscuits. We have excellent reasons for thinking that dogs, bats and moths can detect things that men cannot detect; but these, by themselves, are no reasons for doubting whether men can detect anything at all. We can, in fact, see and hear, among other things, how dogs, bats and moths behave.

Before moving on from this line of disparagement of the senses to the next and much more important line, I want just to give a warning against taking too literally certain pervasive figures of speech. When we speak of our eyes deceiving us, or of the testimony of our noses being suspect, we are talking as if we and our eyes are two parties in a dispute, or as if our noses are in the witness-box while we ourselves are sitting down in the midst of our fellow jurymen. Harm need not come from employing these figures of speech, but it can do so. An athlete might picturesquely lament that his ankle had betrayed him or that his wrist had gone on strike; and if such modes of speech acquired a wide vogue, we might now and then fall into the trap of supposing that we and our limbs are related in the way in which employers are related to their employees. We might start to talk seriously of cricketers being well advised to dismiss their limbs and to try to get on without them.

The notion that our eyes, ears and noses are foreign correspondents who send us messages, which, on examination, turn out often and perhaps always to be fabrications, does enjoy a wide vogue. I think that I need not labour the point that, when taken seriously, it is an attempt to fit familiar generalities about perception, delusions, misestimates, deafness, etc., into an unsuitable conceptual harness, namely that of some political or social fabric, like that of a police-court or the head-office of a newspaper.

People make mistakes, are confused, fail to make things out, overlook things, and so on, in looking about them as they do in calculating, translating, demonstrating and playing games. But only misleadingly can these troubles be described as the outcomes of false or ambiguous messages from reporters. For reporters are themselves good or bad observers, and the critical or uncritical recipients of information from others. So to liken our eyes to reporters is simply to push back the question of the sources of error by one stage—as if there would be some advantage in getting the answer that they were sent false information by *their* eyes and ears or by *their* undisciplined imaginations.

It is now time to turn to a much more difficult and important source of theoretical lawsuits.

As anatomy, physiology and, later, psychology have developed into more or less well-organized sciences, they have necessarily and rightly come to incorporate the study of, among other things, the structures, mechanisms, and functionings of animal and human bodies *qua* percipient. Answers are looked for and found to questions of the general pattern With what organs in our bodies do we see, hear, taste and feel things? and What lesions, diseases and fatigues in these organs diminish or destroy our capacity to see, hear, smell, taste and feel things? Harm need not result, though it can result from formulating the general programme of these inquiries in the question-patterns 'How do we perceive?' and 'Of what is seeing the effect?'

I say that harm can result from so formulating the programme of these inquiries. For these questions, so formulated, easily lend themselves to being construed after the pattern of other familiar and well-behaved questions; and when so construed they worry us by behaving extremely badly. I mean this. The questions 'How do we digest our food?' and 'What happens in us when we drink milk or alcohol?' have discoverable and largely discovered answers. The experts know well enough what happens to the milk or alcohol after we have consumed it and what differences the absorption of them make to our blood-streams, our reaction-times and so on. Doubtless there is more to be found out, but we can think what it will be like to have this extra knowledge. We know where it will fit in.

So when we ask 'How do we see trees?' or 'What happens in us when we see trees?' we are predisposed to expect the same sorts of answers, namely reports of modifications in some of our internal states and processes. Further than that, we are predisposed to think that these reports will tell us not only what happens in us when we perceive but what perceiving is, in the way in which the answer to the question 'What happens in us when we eat poison?' does tell us what being poisoned is. As eating results in nourishment and as haemorrhage results, sometimes, in fainting or in death, so, we fancy, some other external happenings result *via* some other complex internal happenings in the special internal happening of seeing a tree.

Yet, however its details may be filled in, this sort of story leaves us uneasy. When asked whether I do or do not see a tree, I do not dream of postponing my reply until an anatomist or physiologist has probed my insides, any more than he, when asked whether he has seen the zigzag lines on his encephalogram, postpones replying until some other anatomist or physiologist has tested him by a second encephalogram. The question whether I have or have not seen a tree is not itself a question about the occurrence or non-occurrence of experimentally discoverable processes or states some way behind my eyelids, else no one could even make sense of the question whether he had seen a tree until he had been taught complicated lessons about what exists and occurs behind the eyelids.

'No', it might be said 'of course seeing a tree is not just a physiological state or a physiological process. Such states and processes can indeed occur without their owner knowing anything at all about them, where seeing, hearing and smelling belong where remembering, yearning and wondering belong, namely to the field or stream of consciousness. A person can suffer from a vitamin-deficiency without knowing what vitamins are, much less that he is short of them. But he cannot see or remember or wonder without knowing both that he is doing so and what it is that he is doing. These are not bodily states or processes but mental states or processes, and the questions "How do we see trees?" and "What takes place in us when we see trees?" need not anatomical or physiological answers but psychological answers or, perhaps, a conjunction of psychological with physiological answers.'

It is the regular lament of physiologists from Sydenham to Sherrington, not merely that they cannot trace but, worse, that they cannot think how they even might trace the whole chain of processes from the arrival of the initial external physical impulse at the ear-drum, say, the whole way through to the subject detecting the note of a flute. But, the suggestion is, the lament is gratuitous, for somehow, we do not yet know how, the chain of processes at a certain point changes over from having its links in the body to having its latest link or links in the mind. That is where the terminal process has its seat.

There are, I think, a number of objections to this way of retaining our seeings and hearings as the concluding stages of chain-processes while rendering them inaccessible to observation and experimentation in laboratories. But I do not want to go into them here. What I do hope to do is to show that there is something which is drastically wrong with the whole programme of trying to schedule my seeing a tree either as a physiological or as a psychological end-stage of processes. It is not a question of my seeing the tree evading observation and experiment, but of its not being the sort of thing that can be found *or* missed in either the one place or the other. It is not an intractably shy phenomenon, even an introspective phenomenon, because it is not a phenomenon at all. Neither the physiologist nor the psychologist nor I myself can catch me in the act of seeing a tree—for seeing a tree is not the sort of thing in which I can be caught. When I report, perhaps to an oculist, that at a certain moment I saw something, what I report does not qualify to be the filling of any statement of the pattern 'The needle gave me a twinge of pain' or 'His haemorrhage caused him to faint'. To put the point much too crudely, seeing a tree is not an effect —but this is not because it is an eccentric sort of state or process which happens to be exempt from causal explanations but because it is not a state or process at all.

In this one negative respect seeing and hearing are like enjoying. It was partly for this reason that on a former occasion I discussed the notion of enjoyment at such length, namely to familiarize you with the idea that well understood autobiographical verbs can still be grossly misclassified. I argued that some theorists had tried to fit the notions of liking and disliking into the conceptual harness which suits such terms as 'pain' and 'tickle'. They had misclassified *liking* and *disliking* with sensations or feelings. In somewhat the same way, many theorists have tried to subjugate the notions of seeing, hearing and the rest to marching in step either with such notions as *pain* and *tickle*, or else with such notions as *inflammation* or *knee-jerk*. It is tacitly assumed that seeing and hearing must be what stimuli stimulate, only, unfortunately, we have not yet found the way to correlate with these stimuli the perceptions which they stimulate.

I want to satisfy you that verbs like 'see' and 'hear' are not verbs of those sorts. Their functions are quite unlike the functions of verbs like 'tingle', 'wince', 'turn pale' or 'faint'; and answerable questions like 'What made him faint or flinch?' become unaskable questions when 'see' or 'taste' replace 'faint' and 'flinch'.

To begin with, seeing and hearing are not processes. Aristotle points out, quite correctly (*Met.* IX, vi. 7–10) that I can say 'I have seen it' as soon as I can say 'I see it'. To generalize the point that I think he is making, there are many verbs part of the business of which is to declare a terminus. To find something puts 'Finis' to searching for it; to win a race brings the race to an end. Other verbs are verbs of starting. To launch a boat is to inaugurate its career on the water; to found a college is to get it to exist from then on. Now starting and stopping cannot themselves have starts or stops, or, *a fortiori*, middles either. Noon does not begin, go on and finish. It is itself the end of the morning, the beginning of the afternoon and the half-way point of the day. It cannot itself go on for a time, however short. It is not a process or a state. Similarly though we can ask how long a poem is, we cannot ask how long its beginning and end are. They are not sub-stretches of the poem.

We can ask how long it was before the team scored its first goal; or how long the centre-forward spent in manœuvring the ball towards the goal; and even how long the ball was in flight between his kicking it and its going between the goal-posts. But we cannot ask how many seconds were occupied in the scoring of the goal. Up to a certain moment the team was goal-less; from that moment it had scored a goal. But there was no interim moment at which it had half-scored, or scored half of its first goal. Scoring a goal is not a process, but the termination of one and the beginning of another condition of the game. The beginning of a process, such as the start of the motion of an avalanche, is not the cause of that motion; the end of a process, such as the going out of a fire, is the termination but not an effect of the combustion.

It will, I think, be apparent why, with certain reservations, verbs which in this way declare termini cannot be used and are in fact not used in the continuous present or past tenses. The judge may say that he has been trying a man all the morning but not that he has spent the morning or any stretch of the morning in convicting him. I can say that I am occupied in searching for a pencil or trying to solve an anagram, but not that I am occupied in finding the pencil or getting the solution of the anagram. In the same way I can be looking for or looking at something, but I cannot be seeing it. At any given moment either I have not yet seen it or I have now seen it. The verb 'to see' does not signify an experience, i.e. something that I go through, am engaged in. It does not signify a sub-stretch of my life-story.

For safety, let me just mention the reservations. I could certainly say that I was finding misprints all the morning, though not that I was finding some one misprint for any part of that morning. If I found one misprint after another, and the sequence of discoveries went on from breakfast to lunch, then I was finding misprints all the morning. Or, when asked what I am busy about, I could reply that I am occupied in solving anagrams. I have solved some and I have some more which I hope to solve. But I could not say 'I am at present solving this anagram'. Either I have now got the solution or I have not yet got it. In short, a lot of biographical verbs like 'find', 'see', 'detect', and 'solve' share with a lot of other verbs of starting and stopping, which have no special biographical connotations, the negative property of not standing for processes taking place in or to things, or for states in which things remain. The programme, therefore, of locating, inspecting and measuring the process or state of seeing, and of correlating it with other states and processes, is a hopeless programme—hopeless not because the quarry wears seven-leagued boots or a cloak of invisibility, but because the idea that there was such a quarry was the product, almost, of inattention to grammar.

To say that verbs of perceptual detection, unlike those of perceptual exploration, have this resemblance to verbs of stopping and starting is, of course, not to say very much about their business. Checkmating also resembles midnight in this one respect, but a person who knew only this would not know much about checkmating. Let us consider a half-way-house pair of cases. Reaching the end of the measured mile of a race-track takes no time. The runner was running for some five minutes before he reached this point, but his reaching this point did not prolong his running-time. His reaching it is not something with its own beginning, middle and termination. The same is true of winning a mile race. Yet winning involves much more than reaching the end of the measured mile. To win a mile-race, the winner must have been running in competition with at least one other runner; he must not have started before the gun or taken a short-cut or used a bicycle or tripped up his opponent; and he must have reached the end of the measured mile ahead of any opponent. His winning the race comes with his reaching the end of the mile, but to be a victory it has to satisfy quite a lot of additional requirements. Both are attainings, but they are not homogeneous with one another.

Suppose a man, flying in terror from a bull, crossed the start-line of a race-track as the gun was fired, and in his terror reached the tape ahead of the racers. Should we say that he had won the race? or that as he did not know that there was a race on, or anyhow had no intention of matching his speed against anybody save the bull, therefore he was not in the race and so did not win it? Has the careless chess-player whose cuff accidentally pushes his Queen into a square which puts his opponent's King in check-mate, defeated his opponent? We are inclined to require some intention or purpose of a runner or player before we will use the heavily loaded terminus-verbs 'win' and 'checkmate'.

We may imagine an athletics coach with a scientific training researching into the physiology and the psychology of runners. He finds out how men of different bodily builds and different temperaments race over different distances. He finds out the effects of fatigue, of alcohol, of tobacco, of lumbago and of depression upon their performances. He finds out about muscular co-ordination, rhythm, length of stride, and rates of breathing. He finds out about adrenalin, reaction-times and electrical impulses in nerve-fibres. But then he laments that he can find no physiological phenomenon answering to his subject's winning a race, or losing it. Between his terminal output of energy and his victory or defeat there is a mysterious crevasse. Physiology is baffled. Then for a moment our experimentally minded coach cheers up. Perhaps winning and losing are not physiological states or processes having their being under the athlete's skin; perhaps they are mental states or processes, experiences which the athlete himself càn unearth by careful introspection. Indeed this looks very plausible, since runners, who know nothing of what goes on under their own skins, seem often to have no difficulty in discovering that they have won or lost a race. So presumably they discover these facts by introspection upon their mental states and processes. But then, alas, it turns out that this hypothesis will not do either. A runner's victory, though it is tied up, in lots of important ways, with his muscles, nerves and frame of mind, with his early training and the briefing received just before the race, still refuses to be listed among these or kindred phases of his private career. However fast, resolutely and cleverly he has run, he has not won the race unless he had at least one rival, did not cheat and got to the tape first. That these conditions were satisfied cannot be ascertained by probing still further into him. Winning is not a physiological phenomenon, like perspiring or panting, nor yet is it a psychological phenomenon, e.g. an experience like a surge of confidence or a spasm of annoyance. It happens, but, to put it in a way which is not my way, it does not happen in either of those two places, for all that its happening has a great deal to do with what happened in those two places.

In some respects, though certainly not in very many, the verbs 'see' and 'hear' function like the verb 'win'. They do not stand for bodily or psychological states, processes or conditions. They do not stand for anything that goes on, i.e. has a beginning, a middle and an end. The assertion that a subject has seen a misprint carries with it the assertion that there was a misprint for him to see, somewhat as the assertion that a runner has been victorious or defeated carries with it the assertion that there was at least one other runner. The fact that he has seen a misprint has a great deal to do with facts about the light, the condition and position of his eyes and their distance from the page and the absence of screens, the condition of his retina, nerves, etc., the nature of his early education and his present interests, mood and so on. But his seeing or missing the misprint is not itself among the facts about him which can be established in the ways in which these physiological and psychological facts are established. It is not a fact of any of those sorts. None the less, it is not a mysterious fact, any more than winning or losing a race is rendered a mysterious fact by the failure of experiments upon the runner to establish it.

This partial analogy between the business of the verb 'win' and the business of verbs like 'see' and 'hear' of course breaks down quickly and in a number of places. I want to draw attention to two of these collapses, which are, I think, especially illuminating. First, no one would in fact ever suppose that 'winning' stood for a physiological or psychological condition or process, whereas all of us are under strong pressure to assimilate seeing and hearing to having pangs and twinges. Our immunity from the ludicrous blunder which I have invented is partly due to the fact that we know not merely implicitly and in practice, but explicitly and in theory what are the connotations of the verb 'to win'. We were taught the rules of racing when we were taught to race. We not only knew but could say what constituted cheating and not cheating, what constituted competing and what constituted the finish of a race. Even more conspicuously, we had been explicitly taught the rules of chess before we began to use the word 'checkmate'. But verbs of perceiving, though they also carry complex connotations, partly similar to those of 'win' and 'checkmate', were not and could not have been taught to us in this way. We picked up the ways of handling them without being told what these ways were, much as we picked up the pronunciation of the words of our native tongue without any lessons in phonetic theory.

Secondly, whereas the question whether I have won the race, checkmated my opponent or scored a bull's-eye can be decided at least not worse and often better by someone else than by myself, the question whether I have seen or heard something does not ordinarily get or need an umpire. In the vast majority of every-day situations, the person who claims to have found or detected something is excellently placed for upholding that claim. He is as expert an umpire and as favourably situated an umpire as any-one could be. But, and it is an important 'but', not always. The reader who claims to have found a misprint or alternatively to have found a passage correctly printed is not to be trusted if he is a bad speller or not well versed in the language of the passage; the child who claims to see the railway lines meeting just beyond the signal-box is not the person to adjudicate on his claim; and the question whether or not the spectators saw the doves emerging from the conjuror's pocket is for him, not them, to decide. Notice that the conjuror is in a position to reject the claim of the spectators that they saw something happen, if he knows that it did not happen. But if they claim to have seen something happen which did happen, then he cannot, on this score alone, concede their claim. If the thing happened, but happened behind a screen, then their claim to have seen it must be rejected. They could not have seen it unless it happened, and unless it happened in such a place, and at such a distance and in such a light that it was visible to them and unless their eyes were open, properly directed and focused and so on. But when he has conceded that they could have seen it happen, the question whether they did see it happen is not one which he can decide without interrogating them.

What sorts of questions will be put to them? He will not ask them to describe, in retrospect, what experiences they had had, for example what feelings they had felt, what ideas had crossed their minds or what after-images, if any, interfered with their subsequent vision; and of course he will not ask them intricate questions of physiological or psychological sorts, to which they are in no position to give any answers. No answers to such questions would go any way towards deciding whether they had seen what they claimed to have seen. No, he will ask them questions about what they claim to have witnessed happening. If they can tell him facts about the happening which they could not have found out without seeing it happen, their possession of this knowledge is what will satisfy him that they did see it. But sometimes they will not be able to satisfy him in this way, and the question whether they did see what they claimed to see remains undecidable for him. It may also remain undecidable for them too. The anxious mother, listening for the doctor's car, is not sure whether or not she faintly hears the noise of the car a few moments before it does in fact arrive. Perhaps it is imagination—it often is. Perhaps she does just hear it—we often do. But there need be no way of deciding the question after the event.

But in general it is true—we could even say that *of course* in general it is true—that an observer has seen or heard what he says that he has seen or heard. Sometimes he is deceived, for example, by the quickness of the conjuror's hand; but he can be deceived in this abnormal situation only because he is not deceived when witnessing the relatively slow motions of the hands of the people with whom he has ordinarily to do. The child, on his first visit to a skyscraper, may mistakenly judge the vehicles in the street below to be the size of beetles—but for this misestimate to be possible he must have learned to get right, in ordinary situations, the sizes of cars and beetles. The point is

that where winning is the scoring of an athletic success, perceiving is the scoring of an investigational success. We find
things out or come to know them by seeing and hearing. Of
course we know what we have discovered, since to discover that
something is the case is to come to know that it is the case.
Normally, too, though not necessarily, we know how we discovered it, e.g. by sight and not by smell, or by touch and not
by ear; though there are fringe-cases in which we are in doubt
whether we found out that she was angry from the look on her
face or from the tone of her voice; or whether we detected the
proximity of the tree-trunk in the dark from a sort of sudden
thickening in the sounds of things or from a sort of nameless
hint given by the skin of our faces.

In this chapter I have tried to show at least part of the way out
of a certain kind of dilemma about perception. From some well-
known facts of optics, acoustics and physiology it seemed to
follow that what we see, hear or smell cannot be, as we ordinarily
suppose, things and happenings outside us, but are on the contrary, things or happenings inside us. Where we ordinarily speak
confidently of seeing other people's faces, we ought, apparently,
to speak instead of seeing some things going on behind our own
faces, or else, more guardedly, inside our own minds. Where we
ordinarily suppose that we cannot see inside our own heads, and
that only unusually situated surgeons could possibly get a look
at what exists and happens there, we ought instead to allow that
all the sights, sounds, and smells available to us are literally or
else metaphorically internal to us; and that what the surgeon
sees, when peering inside our skulls is, in its turn, nothing that
exists or happens in our skulls but something existing or happening inside his own skull, or else inside some other more
ethereal chamber, totally private to him.
One source of this dilemma is, I have tried to show, the natural
but mistaken assumption that perceiving is a bodily process or
state, as perspiring is; or that it is a non-bodily, or psychological
process or state; or, perhaps, that it is somehow jointly a bodily
and a non-bodily process or state. That is, we have yielded to the
temptation to push the concepts of seeing, hearing and the rest
through the sorts of hoops that are the proper ones for the con-

cepts which belong to the sciences of optics, acoustics, physiology and psychology. The unscheduled but well-disciplined conduct in ratiocination of the notions of seeing, hearing and the rest diverges sharply from the conduct that we have been induced to schedule for them.

To say this is not to disparage the admirable conduct of the concepts of optics, acoustics or physiology. It is no slur on the harness that fits the team-horse to perfection to say that it is an impediment when borrowed for the sleigh-dog. But more than this. There are all sorts of important connexions between the things that we all know, and have to know, about seeing and hearing and the things which have been and will be discovered in the sciences of optics, acoustics, neurophysiology and the rest.

To say that a person's seeing a tree is in principle the same sort of affair as a negative in a camera being exposed, or a gramophone-disc being indented certainly will not do at all. But a great deal has been found out about seeing by working on analogies like this. It is, indeed, the good repute of these discoveries which bribes us to try to subjugate our untechnical generalities about seeing and hearing to the codes that govern so well our technical generalities about cameras, gramophones and galvanometers. Nor is there anything to warn us beforehand whether or where the attempted subjugation will fail.

VIII

FORMAL AND INFORMAL LOGIC

So far the philosophical thickets in which I have rummaged have been thickets that have grown up because of boundary disputes between theories or views which were not themselves philosophers' theories or views. The litigations between the disputants were, necessarily, philosophical troubles, but the original disputants were, for example, mathematicians and men in the street, physiologists and landscape painters, or psychologists and moral instructors.

But now I want to discuss a domestic issue which has fairly recently broken out between certain philosophers and certain philosophically-minded logicians. I shall not do more than give an outline sketch of the situation, since I want to conclude by characterizing against this outline some pervasive features of the variegated thickets in which I have been rummaging.

Since Aristotle, there has existed a branch of inquiries, often entitled 'Formal Logic', which has always adhered more or less closely to general philosophical inquiries. It is not easy to describe this liaison between Formal Logic and philosophy. The systematic presentation of the rules of syllogistic inference is a very different sort of activity from, say, the elucidation of the concept of pleasure. The Aristotle who inaugurated the former is the same thinker as the Aristotle who considerably developed the latter, yet the kinds of thinking in which he was involved are very widely different. The technical problems in the theory of the syllogism have a strong resemblance to the problems of Euclidean geometry; the ideals of systematization and rigorous proof are at work, questions of switches and shades of significance are barred, false moves are demonstrable fallacies. The problems in, say, the theory of pleasure or perception or moral responsibility are not like this. Aristotle debates with Plato and Socrates, and the issues become better defined as the debate progresses, but the debate does not take the shape of a chain of theorems, nor do the arguments used in that debate admit of notational codification. Whether a given philosophical argument is valid or fallacious is, in general, itself a debatable question. Simple inspection cannot decide. More often it is a question of whether the argument has much, little or no force. Yet different though Formal Logic is from philosophy, the operations characteristic of Formal Logic exercise a detectable, if minor, control over the operations characteristic of philosophy. For good or for ill, the ways in which Aristotle debates the notion of *pleasure*, the *soul* or the *continuum* reflect lessons which he had taught himself in his logical inquiries. Nor is Aristotle peculiar in this. With a negligible number of exceptions, every philosopher of genius and nearly every philosopher of even high talent from Aristotle to the present day has given himself some schooling in some parts of Formal Logic, and his subsequent philosophical reasonings have exhibited the effects upon him of this self-schooling, including sometimes his revolts against it.

In some respects the following analogy holds. Fighting in battles is markedly unlike parade-ground drill. The best conducted drill-evolutions would be the worst possible battle-movements, and the most favourable terrain for a rearguard action would entirely forbid what the barrack-square is made for. None the less the efficient and resourceful fighter is also the well-drilled soldier. The ways in which he takes advantage of the irregularities of the ground show the marks of the schooling he had received on the asphalt. He can improvise operations in the dark and at the risk of his life now, partly because he had learned before to do highly stereotyped and formalized things in broad daylight and in conditions of unmitigated tedium. It is not the stereotyped motions of drill, but its standards of perfection of control which are transmitted from the parade-ground to the battlefield.

Aristotelian Formal Logic gave weapon-drill in only a limited variety of rather short-range inference-weapons. The supplementations given by the Megarian and Stoic logicians were, unfortunately, only slightly and belatedly influential. It was left to the nineteenth and twentieth centuries to generalize and systematize the discipline. In particular, the discipline was then in considerable measure mathematicized, and mathematicized in two separate ways. First, the new builders of Formal

Logic, being themselves mathematicians, knew how to give mathematical shape, mathematical rigour and mathematical notations to this branch of abstract theory. Secondly, since their interest in Formal Logic derived from dissatisfaction with the logical foundations of mathematics itself, Formal Logic came to be not only mathematical in style but also mathematical in subject-matter; to be employed, that is, primarily in order to fix the logical powers of the terms or concepts on which hinged the proofs of propositions in pure mathematics.

Formal or Symbolic Logic has grown up into a science or discipline of such scope, such rigour and such fertility that it is now out of all danger of surviving only as the nursery-governess of philosophy. Indeed, philosophers are now complacent if they and their pupils are capable of doing their schoolroom sums in the subject, and gratified and flattered if original logicians are willing to join them, from time to time, in their own expeditions over the moors.

Now, perhaps, I can indicate in a very provisional way the nature of the dispute which has already begun between Formal Logic and general philosophy. Some properly zealous, if sometimes gratuitously jealous Formal Logicians are now beginning to say to the philosopher 'It is time that you stopped trying to solve your problems by your old-fashioned exercises in improvisation and trial-and-error. Your problems are, as you say yourself, logical problems, and we have now got the procedures for solving logical problems. Where you grope, we calculate. Where you haggle, we employ the cash-register. Where you ponder imponderable pros and cons, we work out the correct logical change.'

The natural response of the offended and also jealous philosopher is this. 'Yes, you have invented or hit upon a private game, with fewer pieces but more squares than are provided by chess. You have converted the words "logic" and "logical" to your private ends, and now you invite us to cease exploring the moors in order to become conductors on your trams. And for what? For nothing, apparently, but the proliferation of truistic formulae. No philosophical problem of any interest to anyone has yet been solved by reducing it to the shape or size that suits some slot in your slot-machine. Your cash-register is indeed quite impeccable and totally neutral, and for that reason it cannot be appealed to for aid in the settlement of any bargaining-disputes. There was the notion, once projected by Leibniz and later championed by Russell, that philosophers would soon be so equipped and drilled that they would be able to decide their issues by calculation. But now we have learned, what we should have foreseen, that questions which can be decided by calculation are different, *toto caelo* different, from the problems that perplex. There is one person to whom it is impertinence to give the advice that he should keep one foot on the kerb—and that is the pathfinder. Kerbs cannot exist where the road is unmade, and roads cannot be made where the route has not been found."

You can guess for yourselves the abusive nouns which are now liable to be interchanged. 'Muddler-through', 'romantic', 'anti-scientist', 'hunch-rider', 'litterateur' and of course 'Platonist' come from the one side; from the other side there come 'Formalist', 'computer', 'reductionist', 'pseudo-scientist' and, of course, 'Platonist'.

As might be anticipated, neither party is right, though both are more nearly right than the appeasers who try to blend the operations of the one party with the operations of the other. The drill-sergeant is wrong who thinks that soldiering consists in going through the motions tabulated in the drill-book. The *franc-tireur* is wrong who thinks that soldiering consists in outbursts of amateur gunmanship. But neither is so wrong as the scenario-writer who represents fighting soldiers as heroes going berserk in close column of platoons.

Let us examine, rather more closely, the actual work, as distinct from the intermittent promises of Formal Logicians. Aristotle, it is nearly enough correct to say, examined certain ranges of inferences, namely those which pivot on the notions of *all*, *some*, and *not*. He saw that from two premisses like 'some men are blue-eyed' and 'some men are red-haired' it does not follow that any men are both blue-eyed and red-haired, or, of course, that none are. On the other hand from 'all men are mortal' and 'all philosophers are men' it does follow that all philosophers are mortal. There are rules governing the employment of *all*, *some* and *not* such that all inferences pivoting on two or all three of these concepts, arranged in certain ways, are valid, while all inferences pivoting on them arranged in certain other ways are invalid. These rules are perfectly general, anyhow in this sense, that differences of concrete subject-matter make no difference to the validity or fallaciousness of the inferences. The quantifier-words 'all' and 'some' can be followed indifferently by 'men', 'cows', 'gods' or what you will, without affecting our decision that the inference holds or does not hold. What determines whether a proposed syllogism is valid or fallacious is the work given to 'all', 'some' and 'not', irrespective of the concrete topics of its premisses and conclusion. So, for brevity, we can say that Aristotle was investigating the logical powers of certain topic-neutral concepts, namely those of *all, some* and *not*. These are sometimes listed among what are nowadays called the 'logical constants'.

In a similar way the Megarian and Stoic logicians began the investigation of the logical powers of the equally topic-neutral concepts of *and, or,* and *if*; they concentrated on certain pro-positional conjunctions or connectives, where Aristotle had concentrated on certain quantifiers. They were studying the legitimacy and illegitimacy of possible arguments in so far as they hinged on these particular topic-neutral conjunctions.

These studies yielded a modest degree of codification of the inference-patterns that were examined, and even a semi-Euclideanization of the rules of these inferences. Certain crucial fallacy-patterns were classified. So it was natural, though, as we now know, quite mistaken to suppose that any piece of valid reasoning whatsoever was, by some device or other of re-wording, reducible to one of the already scheduled patterns, and every piece of fallacious reasoning reducible to one of the already registered howlers. Some terms like 'all', 'some' and 'not', and perhaps also 'and', 'or' and 'if' do carry inferences; the rest, it was mistakenly supposed, do not.

Part of what characterizes the terms which do, on this view, carry inferences is that these terms or 'logical constants' are indifferent to subject-matter or are topic-neutral; so part of what characterizes all the other terms which were supposed not to carry inferences is that they are not topic-neutral. Inferences are valid or invalid in virtue of their forms, and to say this, it was supposed, was to say that they were valid or invalid because of the ways in which certain topic-neutral or purely formal expressions occurred in certain positions and arrangements in their premisses and conclusions. This temptingly crisp doctrine, whose obituary notice has yet to be written, might easily suggest the following demarcation of Formal Logic from philosophy. Formal Logic, it might be said, maps the inference-powers of the topic-neutral expressions or logical constants on which our arguments pivot; philosophy has to do with the topical or subject-matter concepts which provide the fat and the lean, but not the joints or the tendons of discourse. The philosopher examines such notions as *pleasure, colour, the future*, and *responsibility*, while the Formal Logician examines such notions as *all, some, not, if* and *or*.

But this way of making the division quickly breaks down. To begin with, topic-neutrality is not enough to qualify an expression as a logical constant. European languages, ancient and modern, and especially the largely uninflected languages, are rich in topic-neutral expressions, most of which have, for very good reasons, received no attention at all from Formal Logicians. We may call English expressions 'topic-neutral' if a foreigner who understood them, but only them, could get no clue at all from an English paragraph containing them what that paragraph was about. Such expressions can or must occur in any paragraph about any topic, abstract or concrete, biographical or legal, philosophical or scientific. They are not dedicated to this topic as distinct from that. They are like coins which enable one to bargain for any commodity or service whatsoever. You cannot tell from the coins in the customer's hand what he is going to buy. In this way 'not', 'and', 'all', 'some', 'a', 'the', 'is', 'is a member of', etc., certainly are topic-neutral, but so are 'several', 'most', 'few', 'three', 'half', 'although', 'because', 'perhaps', 'may', as well as hosts of other conjunctions, particles, prepositions, pronouns, adverbs, etc. Some expressions seem to be nearly but not quite topic-neutral. The temporal conjunctions 'while', 'after' and 'before', and the spatial conjunction 'where' could be used not in all, but only in nearly all sorts of discourse. Our foreigner could tell from the occurrence of temporal conjunctions in the paragraph that no purely geometrical matter was being discussed.

But not only do Formal Logicians very properly ignore the great majority of topic-neutral expressions, as not being in their beat; they also, very properly, bestow their professional attentions upon the logical powers of certain classes of expressions which are by no means topic-neutral. Relational expressions like 'north of', 'taller than' and 'encompasses' are pivots of strict inferences, and it has proved necessary and feasible to divide such expressions up into families according to the sorts of inferences which they do and do not carry. 'Taller-than', for example, is transitive, in the sense that if A is taller than B, and B than C, then A is taller than C. But 'next to' and 'mother of' are not transitive. A can be next to B and B to C without A being next to C; and Sarah cannot be the mother of the child of her own daughter. This does not prevent us from discovering rigorous parities of reasoning between, for example, inferences hinging on 'north of' and inferences hinging on 'encompasses'. But the feature of parity cannot always be detached for separate examination by publication of some elided topic-neutral expression. Sometimes it can. 'Fatter than' works, in some directions, like 'hotter than', and what is common to the two can be brought out by the rewording 'more fat than' and 'more hot than', where the expression 'more so and so than' is a detachable topic-neutral expression.

So we should say, perhaps, with considerable loss of crispness and misleadingness, that Formal Logic is a certain sort of study of parities of reasoning or certain special kinds of parities of reasoning; and that it is convenient, when possible, to exhibit these parities by operations with topic-neutral expressions detached from any particular topical contexts; but that this is not essential and is not always possible. Not all strict inferences pivot on the recognized logical constants, and not all topic-neutral expressions qualify for treatment as logical constants.

A further amendment is required. I have spoken as if our ordinary 'and', 'or', 'if', 'all', 'some' and so on are identical with the logical constants with which the Formal Logician operates. But this is not true. The logician's 'and', 'not', 'all', 'some' and the rest are not our familiar civilian terms; they are conscript terms, in uniform and under military discipline, with memories, indeed, of their previous more free and easy civilian

lives, though they are not living those lives now. Two instances
are enough. If you hear on good authority that she took arsenic
and fell ill you will reject the rumour that she fell ill and took
arsenic. This familiar use of 'and' carries with it the temporal
notion expressed by 'and subsequently' and even the causal
notion expressed by 'and in consequence'. The logicians' conscript 'and' does only its appointed duty—a duty in which 'she
took arsenic and fell ill' is an absolute paraphrase of 'she fell ill
and took arsenic'. This might be called the minimal force of
'and'. In some cases the overlap between the military duties
and the civilian work and play of an expression is even slighter.
What corresponds in the glossary of Formal Logic to the civilian
word 'if' is an expression which plays only a very small, though
certainly cardinal part of the role or roles of that civilian word.

This point that Formal Logic operates (1) only with some,
and not with all topic-neutral expressions, and (2) only with
artificial extracts from the selected few topic-neutral expressions
of ordinary discourse is sometimes used by philosophers as a
criticism of the programme of Formal Logic. Where the philosopher concerns himself with full-blooded concepts like that of
pleasure or *memory*, the Formal Logician concerns himself only
with meatless concepts like those of *not* and *some*; and even these
have to be filed down to reduced size and unnatural shape before
the Formal Logician will deign to inspect them. Moreover, the
philosopher investigates concepts which, in one way or another,
generate genuine perplexities. He investigates the concept, say,
of *seeing* and not that of, say, *perspiring*, since the former is
charged with paradoxes where the latter is not. But, the
criticism goes, the Formal Logician investigates the inference-
carrying labours of concepts which engender no paradoxes whatsoever; what he finds out about *and* and *not* are only elaborations
of what every child has completely mastered in his early talking
years.

I mention this allegation here because it makes the right
opening for me. It is quite false that doing Formal Logic is
doing gratuitous and profitless philosophy upon philosophically
transparent concepts. It is quite false, equally, that the philosopher is doing makeshift and amateurish Formal Logic upon
wrongly chosen because non-logical concepts. The battlefield is

not a makeshift parade-ground; and the parade-ground is not a sham battlefield.

None the less, there remains a very important way in which the adjective 'logical' is properly used to characterize both the inquiries which belong to Formal Logic and the inquiries which belong to philosophy. The Formal Logician really is working out the logic of *and, not, all, some,* etc., and the philosopher really is exploring the logic of the concepts of *pleasure, seeing, chance,* etc., even though the work of the one is greatly unlike the work of the other in procedure and in objectives. Neither is doing what the other is doing, much less is either doing improperly what the other is doing properly. Yet we are not punning when we say, for example, that the considerations which are decisive for both are 'logical' considerations, any more than we are punning if we say that the choice of drill-evolutions and the choice of battle-evolutions are both decided by 'military' considerations. How can this be?

I find the following partial parallel of some assistance. Trading begins with barter of goods for goods, and, by means of fixed places and times for markets, such barter-dealings can reach a fairly high degree of systematization. Though the relative exchange-values of different sorts of goods vary with times and places, some measure of stabilization can be achieved by tacit or explicit convention. There is, however, even at this stage, a strong pressure upon traders to use just a few kinds of consumable goods not only for consumption, but also, at least for a short time, as a sort of informal currency. Dried fishes, cigarettes or iron bars, though wanted for use, come also to be wanted because any other trader can be relied on to accept them, whether he himself wants to use them or not, because they will always be exchangeable anywhere for consumable goods. So long as they are reasonably imperishable, easy to store and handle, easy to count or weigh, and certain to be wanted some day by someone for consumption purposes, they are negotiable as exchange-tokens. From this stage to the stage of operating with a conventional currency or legal tender is a relatively short step. Though no one, perhaps, can be expected to want to use metal discs for any consumption purpose, everyone can be expected to want to use them for exchange-purposes. They might be described as auxiliary goods, goods which are of little or no utility in themselves, but of great utility for getting and disposing of other goods which are wanted for themselves.

For future purposes we should notice another kind of auxiliary goods. Baskets, pitchers, sacks, brown paper and string are, to exaggerate a little, of no use in themselves, but only for the collection and housing of goods which we do want for themselves. But clearly the way in which baskets and string are auxiliary to marketing and storing is different from the way in which coins are auxiliary. A basket or keg is only being actually useful to us when we are in possession of goods for it to contain. A coin is useful to us in another way. While we possess the coin, we do not possess what we shall buy with it. But still there is a certain similarity between them. A coin is commodity-neutral, for I can buy any sort of commodity with it. A sack or a piece of string is, in lower degree, commodity-neutral. You cannot tell from the fact that I go to market with a sack or some string precisely what kinds of goods I shall bring back with its aid. It would be useful for any of a fairly wide range of goods, though not, of course, for all kinds of goods.

Linguistic dealings between men have some of the features of market-dealings between men. There is a comparable pressure upon language to evolve idioms, which may or may not be separate words, to subserve in stabilized ways different kinds of constantly recurring linguistic negotiations. We need and therefore we get a variety of topic-neutral words, inflections, constructions, etc., some of which function rather like baskets, pitchers, string and wrapping-paper, while others function rather like the dried fishes, cigarettes or iron bars and, later on, rather like the coins and currency notes, part or the whole of whose utility is to serve as instruments of exchange.

There arises, I suppose, a special pressure upon language to provide idioms of this latter kind, when a society reaches the stage where many matters of interest and importance to everyone have to be settled or decided by special kinds of talk. I mean, for example, when offenders have to be tried and convicted or acquitted; when treaties and contracts have to be entered into and observed or enforced; when witnesses have to be cross-examined; when legislators have to draft practicable measures and defend them against critics; when private rights and public duties have to be precisely fixed; when complicated commercial arrangements have to be made; when teachers have to set tests to their pupils; and, by no means earliest, when theorists have to consider in detail the strengths and weaknesses of their own and one another's theories.

Those topic-neutral words of natural languages which are nearest to the officially recognized logical constants roughly coincide, perhaps, with the best consolidated exchange-auxiliaries that our native tongues have provided. They exist to be negotiating instruments. The conscript expressions actually used by Formal Logicians, together with the methodically designed expressions of mathematics, correspond in many respects with a legal tender. A sentence with one or more 'logical words' in it, is a sentence with one or more price-tickets on it. Other topic-neutral words, inflections, etc., correspond more closely with the paper, string, sacks and pitchers with which we go to and return from the market.

Now perhaps we are in a position to see more clearly some of the ways in which the Formal Logician's interests are unlike those of the philosopher and yet not entirely separate. The ordinary person is much concerned both with the domestic or consumption-utility of different goods and also, as a marketer, with their exchange-values, i.e. what they can be got for or what they would fetch; and these considerations vary with every different kind and quantity of goods. No such problems exist for the bank clerk about the coins that he takes in and gives out. A sixpenny-bit buys whatever costs sixpence, and its purchasing power stands to the purchasing power of a penny or a half-crown in known and fixed relations. Its value is stamped on its face.

Somewhat similarly there is and can be no incertitude about the exchange-values of the numerals of simple arithmetic or the conscript logical constants of the Formal Logician, since they have been designed or chartered to do just what they do. Nor can there be much incertitude about the inference-carrying powers of such vernacular words as 'not', 'some', 'and' and 'or', since their prime business is to make negotiations decidable.

Where the philosopher has to investigate both the special content of, say, the concepts of *enjoying* and *remembering* and their kinds of logical behaviour, the logician does not have to investigate his semi-technical concepts of *and* and *not*. Their work is what they are chartered to do, and he drew up their charters or at least has read them. On the other hand, a special theoretical task does remain for him to do. Much as arithmetic and algebra have problems of their own, which begin when the elementary use of numbers in counting is mastered, so the Formal Logician has his analogous problems, which begin long after the elementary mastery is achieved of his chartered *all, some* and *not*; *and, or, if* and the rest. His occupational problems are not how to determine the exchange-equivalents of his logical constants, but how to derive some from others, to establish, that is, the principles of the calculation of them. His task is to incorporate them in a sort of Euclidean deductive system. The experienced but uneducated bus-conductor could write down the beginning of an endless list of the correct change that can be given for different coins and handfuls of coins, but to do this would not be to do arithmetic. The accountant, unlike our bus-conductor, must know how to calculate, and some other experts must have developed the science which the accountant applies.

The topic-neutral expressions of our natural language which are the civilian counterparts to the conscript logical constants do not behave quite as their conscript counterparts behave, though the differences are sometimes slight and sometimes not troublesomely gross. For obvious reasons, logicians have conscripted only the soldierly-looking civilians and, as we have seen, there are good reasons why the languages of highly organized societies provide a certain number of decision-facilitating expressions.

But most of the terms of everyday and technical discourse are not like coins or even like cowrie-shells. They are like consumption-goods, which can, indeed, be traded for and traded with. But their barter-values are not stamped upon their faces. They can, for the most part, be the hinges of legitimate and illegitimate inferences; there are parities of reasoning between inferences pivoting on one of them and inferences pivoting on some others of them; but there is, ordinarily, no way of extracting from them some implicit logical constant or web of logical constants to be credited with the carriage of those inferences—any more than there is really an invisible half-crown lurking inside a bag of potatoes which renders these potatoes the barter-equivalent of a basket of fruit or a couple of lobsters.

They have their logical powers or barter-values, but they are not to be read off the terms of their official charters, since they have no charters. The philosopher's problem is to extract their logical powers from the dealings which we transact with them, somewhat as the phonetician has to extract the principles of phonetics from the ways in which we have learned to pronounce our words—though the method and purposes of the extraction are hugely different.

How then, it remains to be asked, is the philosopher a client of the Formal Logician? Part of the answer I have already suggested. To know how to go through completely stereotyped movements in artificial parade-ground conditions with perfect correctness is to have learned not indeed how to conduct oneself in battle but how rigorously to apply standards of soldierly efficiency even to unrehearsed actions and decisions in novel and nasty situations and in irregular and unfamiliar country.

Or, which is not quite the same thing, it is rather like what geometry is to the cartographer. He finds no Euclidean straight hedgerows or Euclidean plane meadows. Yet he could not map the sinuous hedgerows that he finds or the undulating meadows save against the ideally regular boundaries and levels in terms of which alone can he calculate out the relative positions and heights of the natural objects which he is to record from the visual observations that he makes. The cartographer is one of the clients of geometry. The possibility of his map being approximately correct or precise is the gift of Euclid. So is the possibility of his reading off his map distances, areas and bearings which he did not measure when constructing his map.

Or, lastly, it is what accountancy is to the merchant, who, though his problems are not arithmetical problems, still, in his handling of them, needs the constant back-room check of the properly balanced ledger. The trader is a client of the accountant.

But patently fighting cannot be reduced to drill, cartography cannot be reduced to geometry, trading cannot be reduced to balancing accounts. Nor can the handling of philosophical problems be reduced to either the derivation or the application

of theorems about logical constants. The philosopher is perforce
doing what might be called 'Informal Logic', and the suggestion
that his problems, his results or his procedures should or could
be formalized is as wildly astray as would be the corresponding
suggestions about the soldier, the cartographer and the trader.
We could go further and say that the whole point of drill, of
geometry, of accountancy and of Formal Logic would be gone if
they could be completely dissociated from their clients. It would
be like reserving the roads for the sole use of steam-rollers, or
like forbidding all trade save money-changing.

What I have been trying to think out during the course of these
lectures is the ways in which live problems in Informal Logic are
forced upon us, willy-nilly by the interferences which are unwittingly committed between different teams of ideas. The
thinker, who is also Everyman, learns, *ambulando*, how to
impose some measure of internal order and logical discipline
upon the players in his different conceptual teams. What he does
not learn *ambulando* is how to contrast and co-ordinate team with
team; how, for example, to contrast and co-ordinate what he
knows about seeing and hearing with what he finds out in the
course of developing his optical, acoustic, and neurophysio-
logical theories; or how to contrast and co-ordinate what he
knows about our daily control of things and happenings in the
world with what he knows about the implications of truths in
the future tense; or how to contrast and co-ordinate what he
knows about the everyday furniture of the mundane globe with
the conclusions of his theories about the ultimate constitution of
matter.

Let me bring together some specific points which I have tried
to illustrate. I think that they hang together.

First, we are under no pressure to examine the logical behaviour of isolated concepts, selected at random, perhaps, from
a dictionary. We have no special puzzles about the notions of
perspiration, *off-side* or *taxation*. The pressure comes when we
find (for instance) that the things which we know well are the
right sorts of things to say with verbs like 'see' and 'hear' and
all the others of that not very well defined family seem to be put
out of court by, or else to put out of court, the things which we

also know well are the right sorts of things to say with expressions like 'optic nerve', 'neural impulse', 'light-waves' and all the rest of their not very well-defined families. Our characteristic questions are not questions in the logical statics of insulated and single concepts, but questions in the logical dynamics of apparently interfering systems of concepts.

Consequently to understand the work of an original philosopher it is necessary to see—and not merely to see but to feel—the logical *impasse* by which he was held up. We should always be asking the question Just what was the conceptual fix that he was in? What dilemma was pinching him? Nor is it always easy to identify or describe this *impasse*, since he himself would seldom, if ever, be able to diagnose his trouble. To be able to diagnose it would be to be half way out of it. To him, while in the trouble, the situation feels like that of a man in a fog whose left foot feels securely planted on the solid bank, and whose right foot feels securely planted on a reliable boat—and yet the bank and the boat seem to move independently. He cannot lift either foot from its foothold and yet he cannot, it seems, keep his feet together.

Kant, to take a particular example, wholeheartedly believed in Newtonian physics; he also wholeheartedly believed in the autonomy of morals. Yet the Laws of Motion seemed to leave no room for the Moral Law, and the absolute obligation for men to act in certain ways, and therewith the possibility of their doing so seemed to leave no room for the physical necessity of the motions of all, including human, bodies. Neither the truths of science nor the truths of morals could be abandoned, yet each seemed to disqualify the other.

Parallel with this *impasse* or rather, as I think, subterranean to it was another deeper and wider crevasse. Mechanical principles contain the explanations of all bodily states and processes. But plants, insects, animals and men are bodily organisations. So all their states and processes can be mechanically explained. Yet living things are not merely complex mechanisms; the biological sciences are not mere off-shoots of mechanics. Where there is life there is purposiveness, and where there is sentient, mobile and, especially, conscious and intellectual life there are progressively higher and higher levels or types of purposiveness.

The biologist, the zoologist and the psychologist must conduct their inquiries as if they were vitalists, even though they feel intellectual obligations to pay lip-service to mechanism. So Kant, and not Kant alone, had one foot securely planted on the solid bank of Newtonian mechanics, and the other foot securely planted on the boat of a semi-Aristotelian vitalism.

It is sometimes suggested that Kant set himself the tasks of analysing a heap of concepts, such as *space, time, causation, duty, life,* and *purpose*. But this would be misleading in at least two important ways. First, he did not set himself these tasks; they set themselves to him. Secondly, they did not attack him in a random sequence of local raids; they were the spearheads of a concerted offensive from two flanks. His tactics against these several units had and had to have a strategy behind them.

Next, I hope to have shown that the settlement or even partial settlement of a piece of litigation between theories cannot be achieved by any one stereotyped manœuvre. There is no one regulation move or sequence of moves as a result of which the correct logical bearings between the disputing positions can be fixed. This is not to say that we may not often discern or seem to discern some fairly broad similarities of pattern between one dilemma and another; and these may sometimes suggest ways of tackling the one issue on the analogy of ways which have been effective in tackling the other. But such broad analogies may be hindrances as well as helps. A darling model may in a new application work like a Procrustean bed.

To say this is to say, in another way, that the hope that philosophical problems can be, by some stereotyped operations, reduced to standard problems in Formal Logic is a baseless dream. Formal Logic may provide the exploratory Informal Logician with a compass by which to steer, but not with a course on which to steer and certainly not with rails to obviate steering. Where there is virgin forest, there can be no rails; where rails exist the jungle has long since been cleared.

None the less, the debating operations by which alone the Informal Logician can move are controlled by logical considerations, even though not, save pretty indirectly, by considerations of Formal Logic. There is, for example, at least some force in the argument that to enjoy doing something cannot be a case of a sensation of some sort being set up in the agent by his action, since acute sensations distract the attention from everything else than those sensations, whereas great enjoyment goes with complete absorption in the activity enjoyed; and such force as there is in this argument works directly towards some grasp of the cross-bearings between the concepts of *pleasure, activity, attention* and *feeling*.

A little while ago I distinguished between everyday civilian concepts and the conscript concepts with which the Formal Logician and the mathematician operate. I said that the functions of the latter were to be read off their charters, where the conduct in inference of the former could not be read off their charters, since they were under no charters. But a reservation has to be made for the technical terms of specialisms like games, sciences and professions. The rules for the employment of these terms are, in some degree, explicit. A person who has mastered the apparatus to which they belong knows enough to be able to state, sometimes with great precision, what the job of one of them is with relation to the jobs of the rest of them. Their team-roles are more or less well inter-defined.

It follows, what seems to be true in fact, that the employer of such officially incorporated terms, is ordinarily embarrassed by few, if any, perplexities in the course of his regular, technical use of them. But there are two kinds of situation in which even he, and especially he can be embarrassed. The first is when the theory, business or other activity which the apparatus subserves is itself in process of major development or change—when, that is, the roles of all or most of the members of the apparatus are being enlarged or twisted. If the property-laws of a state are being stretched to cover countless different kinds of Crown property, State property, and the property of nationalized industries and of chartered public companies, then the lawyer himself will, for a time, find himself divided between the old and the new forces of his own technical dictions. When Auction Bridge was giving place to Contract Bridge, or when Association Football was breeding Rugby Football, or when geometry was absorbing non-Euclidean geometries or when 1953 physical theory is growing away, in some directions, from 1943 physical theory, the regular or habitual functions of many of the technical

terms employed fall short of their new functions; and their
employer feels doubts, for the time being, whether he is not
playing fast and loose with their *real* meanings, namely those
that he learned long ago. Yesterday's impossibilities are today's
possibilities, yet are not these prohibited by the well-known
rules? Surely it is still *really* a foul to pick up the football with
the hands?

The second situation in which the employer of a technical
apparatus of internally well-disciplined terms may be perplexed
about their employment is, in general, the more important. This
is the situation in which he is required to discuss inter-theory
questions, questions, that is, whose answers are not contributions to the body of his theory, but are, instead, contributions to
the understanding of the gist and drift of his theory by outsiders,
whether they be thoughtful citizens at large, or themselves the
sponsors of other special theories. This is the situation of the
lawyer debating with the ordinary citizen, or with the psychologist or with the political reformer; or it is the situation of the
theologian debating with the astro-physicist or the geneticist or
with the ordinary citizen. In such situations perfect internal
control of the concepts of his theory is compatible with the
greatest embarrassment in marrying his occupational dictions
with the occupational or public dictions of his interlocutor.
Indeed, to strike a pessimistic note, the more at home he is with
his specialized conceptual apparatus, the less capable will he be
apt to be of operating outside of it. What work so well during
his daily employment must, he will feel, be the proper implements to employ elsewhere. Of course diplomatic negotiations
can best be conducted in the well-tried idioms of the Stock
Exchange, the Trade Union, the regiment or the chapel.

The point here is that, odd though it sounds, an intelligent
man may both know perfectly how to put a concept to its
regular work within its appropriate field of employment, and
thus have complete mastery of its domestic logical duties and
immunities, and yet be quite at a loss to determine its external
or public logic. He can, perhaps, think lucidly as a geometrician
and still be perplexed about the relations between geometrical
points and pencilled dots on paper or molecules or atoms; or he
can, perhaps, think lucidly as an economist and still be perplexed

about the identity or non-identity of his marginal farmer, with this or that unprosperous smallholder. Ability to use the private lingo of a theory does not necessarily carry with it the ability to render this lingo into public dictions which are neutral between theories. It is often the very powerfulness of the domestic logic of a well-organized theory or discipline which engenders the litigations between it and other theories or, perhaps more often, between it and common knowledge. For it is just to this well-known drill that the thinker who has been trained in it feels obliged to try to subjugate the members of these other conceptual teams.

So what I hope to have done is to have brought out for examination some features of what I have dubbed the 'informal logic' of our ordinary and our technical concepts; and shown how questions about this informal logic are forced upon us by the unanticipated and unpreventable quarrels which break out from time to time between one team of ideas and another. What is often, though not very helpfully, described as 'the analysis of concepts', is rather an operation—if you like a 'synoptic' operation—of working out the parities and the disparities of reasoning between arguments hinging on the concepts of one conceptual apparatus and arguments hinging on those of another. The need to undertake such operations first makes itself felt only when some dilemma shows its horns.

Printed in the United States
1065000001B/315